Busy Living

To Nicola
with every blessing!
[signature]

Busy Living

Blessing not Burden

Emma Ineson

continuum

Continuum

The Tower Building
11 York Road
London SE1 7NX

80 Maiden Lane
Suite 704
New York, NY 10038

www.continuumbooks.com

First published 2007

British Library Cataloguing-in-Publication Data
A catalogue record for this book is available from the British Library.

ISBN 0 8264 9117 0

Typeset by YHT Ltd, London
Printed and bound by MPG Books Ltd, Bodmin, Cornwall

Contents

To Mat, Molly and Toby
with love

and to Hilary Ineson
who showed me that it is possible to be
a wife, mother, minister, feminist, worker and a Christian
all at the same time.

Acknowledgements

My thanks go to Carolyn Armitage for realizing that there was potential in this subject – and in encouraging me to write about it. I am very grateful to the churches and communities I have been privileged to be part of – St Stephen's Selly Park, Trinity Theological College, Christ Church Dore, Lee Abbey Devon and St Matt's Kingsdown – each of which in their different ways taught me so much about myself, about God and about what it means really to live together. Thank you to Marlene Parsons from Birmingham Diocese who was visionary enough to realize that a married couple with children could both be priests and to John Nolland and David Gillet who encouraged us in that journey. I have had some great colleagues with whom I have thoroughly enjoyed working, especially Chris Turner, David Williams and Chris Edmondson. Wise and valued friends have kept me sane and made me laugh a lot, especially Drew and Elena and David and Jackie. Without the help and support of Barbara and Tony, not a lot of living life to the full would have been possible. Thank you to Molly and Toby, whom I love to distraction. You have kept me busy but happy and the best thing in the world is being your mummy. My principal thanks go to my husband Mat who has been my greatest fan and keenest critic and a wonderful partner in every aspect of life and ministry. I couldn't have done anything without you.

Having it all? 1

This is not a book for people who want to be less busy. It is a book for people who are busy, enjoy it, but want to be able to stay sane in their busyness. It is a book for busy-philes who want to grow and flourish in their relationships with God and the people around them. It is for people who enjoy fulfilling different roles in life – at work, at home, at church – and yet sometimes feel a rising sense of panic at the sheer amount of things they have let themselves in for.

When I was a teenager in the 1980s, we took it for granted that we could 'have it all'. Our mothers had fought for their rights to contraception, promotion, equal pay and childcare. My mother worked and raised me and my sister, some of the time as a single parent. My friends all had mothers who worked, looked after their families and had full social lives. Our role models were women who were successful in all areas of their lives. They were probably also exhausted most of the time, but we didn't realize that back then.

So we did it too. Most of my friends from university days are married and have several children each. Many of us have successful careers in the media, in law, in finance. Some of us are Christians. Some of us are vicars. Some of us are married to vicars. Most of us juggle career, children, partners, friends, God and church. Most of us try to find some time to stay fit, eat well, decorate our houses and go on holiday. Most of us try to keep up meaningful relationships with family and friends. Most of us are worn out.

I have a friend who has a diary on which is written 'I'm a woman. I'm invincible. And I'm tired.' That's how many people feel – and not just women. Men too are busier than ever being fathers, lovers, workers, players, followers of Christ and probably churchwardens on top of it all. But the busyness phenomenon seems to affect women more than men. When I spoke to my husband about this book and about how many women feel guilty about being too busy, he said, 'I think that's a female thing more than a male thing. Women feel guilty that they're too busy. Men feel happy that they're active and useful.'

Statistics back up his view. According to market-research analysts Mintel, two-thirds of women would express the view that 'there are not enough hours in the day', 51 per cent of women describe themselves as busy compared with only 35 per cent of men. Maybe men don't own up to it in surveys, but I know plenty of men who are very busy and would consider themselves to be under pressure much of the time. Maybe it's just not manly to admit it.

Being busy can be good, productive and life-giving. Many people I speak to are busy but wouldn't really want it any other way. However, being *too* busy can also be indicative of a deeper sense of personal malaise. Being too busy can lead me to ask major questions about my priorities, because how I spend my time often exemplifies how I attribute importance to the various aspects of my life. Stopping to ask what my activities say about my priorities is not always a comfortable process. Being over-busy can lead me also to examine my deepest sense of who I am – my identity, my sense of self. If I spend all my life simply running to keep up, what does that say about who I am deep down? No wonder you often hear people cry, 'Stop the world. I want to get off!'

How have we got to this place where everything is open to us, where we are invited to 'have it all', and yet life seems busier and harder than ever? Why at this, of all times, are we finding it more challenging than ever to work out who we really are and what our priorities in life should be? Is it really possible to 'have it all' without losing the plot?

Being a follower of Jesus often doesn't seem to make it any easier. Didn't he say, 'I have come that you might have life and have it to the full' (Jn 10.10 NIV[1])? But following him sometimes just seems to add extra pressure to our already stretched existence and he may as well have said, 'I have come that you might be very, very busy.'

I firmly believe there has to be a solution. God made us social, loving and resourceful people, designed to work, to rest, to play and to worship. In God's plan, it must fit, all this stuff. There must

1. All quotations are from the New Revised Standard Version unless otherwise stated.

be somewhere, somehow, the possibility of leading a fulfilled and happy life that includes all the elements of work, family, leisure, rest, worship and play. And it must be accessible to ordinary men and women, with jobs, friends, colleagues and families.

So how do we do it? If it's not possible to have it all, can I at least have most of it? And can I stay sane in the process? This book is all about making choices. It is about standing above the chaos and working out your priorities. It's about trying to make sense of what you do in your life, with a godly perspective on all the activities and options before you. It's also about surviving – and thriving – as you do so.

Busy living

This is not just a book I've been writing, it's a book I've been living. When I look back on my life so far, all 37 years and 7 months of it, the overriding feeling is that it's been great, but it's been very busy. I haven't stopped. I have had so many opportunities that I am grateful for. I went to school (some of it in Kenya, some in South Wales), I took a gap year, I went to university where I met my husband. We married when I was 22 and our daughter was born when I was 25, by which time I'd finished a master's degree and had started on a PhD. My maternity leave was spent writing my doctoral thesis. We ran youth camps in our holidays and church services at weekends. We had been married for three years when God called both of us at the same time to ordination. We had a young child and didn't know any other couples who were ordained at the same time. We thought God must be joking. He wasn't. We went to theological college together for three years. By the age of 30 I was a priest with a doctorate, an ordained husband, a daughter and another baby on the way, doing a job-shared curacy (the first couple in our diocese to do so). A short maternity leave was fitted in somewhere between Christmas and Easter.

After curacy, we started another job-share at a Christian

conference centre and community at Lee Abbey in Devon. It was meant to be a place of quiet and reflection, and, for the guests who came week by week, mercifully, it was. But for those of us who worked behind the scenes, organizing the conferences and catering for the needs of the guests, it was often a place of busyness and pressure. Much of our role at Lee Abbey involved leading conferences and retreats on developing and maintaining a strong spiritual life. We spent a lot of time praying with other people about their relationships with God. Sometimes I realized I'd been busily helping other people to have a healthy spiritual life when my own really needed a doctor.

It was at Lee Abbey that I first began to reflect on this busyness thing. I realized that I actually quite liked being busy. I have loved everything that I have done with my life so far. Although it might be easy to conclude I've been a bit mad for trying to fit so much in, I wouldn't have had it any other way. I am proud of my achievements. I am delighted with my children and so grateful that I have been in a line of work that has enabled me to combine motherhood with my vocation as a priest.

Yet I am still left with this nagging question: 'Is it really OK to be so busy?'

There have been moments of real stress, where it has felt like it will all come crashing down around me at any moment. A couple of years ago I spent some months very ill with a condition that no one could quite diagnose. (I will return to the issue of illness and busyness later in the book.) Many people said my illness was probably stress related.

There have been periods when hearing God's voice in the midst of it all has been a struggle, when I have yearned to find that pattern of living and working and praying which is 'life in all its fullness', when I have tried to make it all fit better. And yet I have been so happy. Increasingly I have come to realize that busyness is just a natural part of my life, as it is for many people.

Things have changed a bit in the last few months. We've moved away from Lee Abbey and with this move has come a monumental decision. Following a shared path of exploring vocation, being ordained together and two job-shares (during which we've also shared the care of our two children), this time we're doing things differently. Mat has a job as a vicar of a church and I have decided not to look for a paid job initially. That has not been an easy decision for me, as so much of my identity has been bound up in what I do. So this time I'm doing bits and pieces – a bit of writing, a bit of speaking, a bit of mentoring, a bit of pastoral work. I still seem to be just as busy, but the process of consciously deciding, as a couple, what to do and what not to do has led to some serious reflection on my part about what my priorities are and how to stand above the busyness and make some informed decisions. It is some of that reflection that I share with you in this book.

Maybe you are busy (perhaps that's why you've picked up this book). Maybe you are wondering how you will keep juggling all that your life holds on a daily basis. Maybe you would like to take a step back and ask some searching questions of your busyness.

There are so many books by Christian leaders who *used* to have problems but are all right now: 'I used to have a problem with bad thoughts, but now I've conquered them!', 'I used to be busy, but now I've discovered how to slow down!', 'I used to be a workaholic, but now I'm a hermit!', 'I used to be a hopeless wretch, but now I'm great!'. This is not a book like that, written by someone who has got it all sussed, thank you very much. This book is more akin to those websites where fellow sufferers share experiences of their illness. It's shared with you from the middle of it all, when I'm wrestling with the whole thing, rather than afterwards when I've got it all sorted out. I struggle with busyness too. I enjoy it most of the time, but sometimes it feels like a problem. I hope this book will be an encouragement that you're not alone in finding busyness an enjoyable challenge. I hope it might give you one or two ideas about how to do things differently. I hope it will help you to make some wise choices. I hope it will help you to be happier and more confident in who you are and in what you are doing.

My aim in writing it is to help you to live life to the full, to step out in confidence into doing what God calls you to in all areas of your life, but without feeling overwhelmed in the process. The aim is also to help men and women to explore together how a better sense of partnership in all areas of life might lead to liberation of time, energy and resources.

Messages

None of us makes choices in a vacuum. Our values are consciously or subconsciously formed by those around us. We are highly influenced by other people's expectations, whether people we know or people we don't. Every day messages are fired at us about how we should think and act and behave. Consciously or subconsciously we evaluate all of this 'stuff' that comes at us from every direction; from conversations with our friends, TV programmes we watch, articles we read or sermons we hear. It is important to listen to the cultural messages that we are receiving – from our friends, from the media, from the cultures around us, from the church – and to weigh the merit of all these different voices. As Christians we need the ability and the discernment to hear the messages and see the good in them. We also need the strength to weigh and reject that which is not good for us. Because, like it or not, we are influenced by these messages:

> We're caught in a bind: we get quite a lot of exhilaration and sense of freedom from our choices – to be fashionable or stylish, live in the city or the country, be married or stay single. Such decisions are crucial to establishing our identity. But we can't escape the fact that all these choices are made in a context, and the idea that we can identify pure preferences that express our innermost souls is absurd.[2]

Having it all

One of the messages that has come loud and clear for the past 40 years is that it is possible to 'have it all'. Today's 30-somethings have been brought up believing that we can, if not have it all, at least have most of it.

The phrase 'having it all' was first used in the heyday of the

2. Geraldine Bedell, 'What makes women happy?', *Observer*, 11 June 2006.

feminist 1960s by the then editor of *Cosmopolitan* magazine, Helen Gurley. As women increasingly broke free from the stereotypical shackles that suggested that their lot in life was simply to get married and have children, more and more women embraced work and life outside the home. Women were told that now they could do anything. It was perfectly possible to 'have it all', to combine being a mother and working outside the home.

The idea that it is possible to combine career, marriage and family is still alive and well, at least amongst younger women. A recent survey in *Company* magazine, which polled more than 1,000 unmarried young women, found that the average woman (or at least those who respond to questionnaires in *Company* magazine) wants to be settled in a relationship by 28, own her own home by 30, get married at 31 and have her first child at 32, as well as reaching the top of her chosen career by the age of 37. Seven in 10 women said they intended to return to work after having a baby. Only 12 per cent of female readers expected their other half to be the main breadwinner in the family.[3]

However, as everyone has become more and more busy, there are those women, mostly of my generation – in their thirties and forties – who have come to the conclusion that to 'have it all' is simply to 'do it all', and to find oneself wrung out in the effort. Melanie Phillips sums up this view when she writes in the *Daily Mail* (not known as a bastion of women's rights): 'Women themselves are indicating more and more that "having it all" exerts too big a price. Juggling work and motherhood can leave women shredded with exhaustion.'[4] As I pick up my son from school I meet many mothers who have given up successful careers, not necessarily because they wanted to, but because the pressures of juggling work and home life became too much to cope with. For many of them, making that choice has been necessary, but not necessarily easy. In an interview for *The Times*, the editor of *Cosmopolitan* magazine Lorraine Candy says of her readership: 'I was very struck by the fact that a huge number of women cried twice a week. They did not want to be fabulously wealthy. They

---

3. Results of a survey in *Company* magazine, October 2006.
4. Melanie Phillips, 'Having it all', *Daily Mail*, 29 December 2005.

had so much choice and they just wanted to be happy with the choices they made.'[5]

Ah, the choices they've made. That's the crux of it. It would be so much simpler if we didn't have choices. We have many options available to us now:

> As a result, we frequently try to avoid choosing at all, as if it might be possible somehow to have a full-time job, and children, and a good relationship, and friends, and a tidy house, and be thin, and wear the right clothes, and eat in the right restaurants, and possibly be having a really sexy affair as well, complete with suitable underwear ... the more we achieve, the more the horizons of achievement stretch away. And we're completely strung out and not actually doing anything properly.[6]

Partnership and sacrifice

Partnership

The way we work, live and raise our families has changed, largely for the better. However, the changes have not always been supported by a well-reasoned critique of what they mean for Christian men and women. What has been left is confusion about what it means to be a Christian man or a Christian woman today. So has feminism failed Christian men and women? Has the encouragement to have it all simply led to worn-out women, disempowered men and collapsing families?

The conservative right would say it has and the answer is to go back to traditional roles, 'the old way of doing things' where occupation was prescribed according to gender – women at home, men in leadership in family and church. I don't think it's as simple as that. Of course for some people that is the best option, but the

---

5. Interview with Ruth Gledhill, 'Show a little spirit', *The Times*, 6 March 2004.
6. Geraldine Bedell, 'What makes women happy?', Observer, June 11, 2006.

awkward fact is that for others God puts a spanner into the works of that nice, neat scenario by calling women to be priests, or lawyers, or teachers, and by calling some men to be primary childcarers. The answer isn't to go back to the old-fashioned way of doing it, but for men and women to learn to hear each other's voices in the busyness – to be partners in the way intended by God from the start and described in Genesis 1, and to make decisions and choices together at all levels of society.

If we were to foster better communication between the sexes, better understanding of what it means to be called to this life or that, and a degree of sacrifice on both sides, we might come close to a way of life which was manageable for both sexes – full, active, busy, but enjoyable.

Partnership between men and women in both the public and domestic spheres is a godly imperative. The 'big story' of Christianity is that Christ came to redeem fallen humanity and that we are to work with him towards a restoration of the ideal state for humankind that God intended. One of the things we are to work to redeem is the partnership between men and women at all levels of life and work.

In the beginning there was partnership between women and men in procreation and in work. When God created Adam and Eve and placed them in the Garden he told *both* to be involved with having children ('be fruitful and multiply') and he told *both* to work ('fill the earth and subdue it'):

> So God created humankind in his image, in the image of God he created them; male and female he created them. God blessed them, and God said to them, 'Be fruitful and multiply, and fill the earth and subdue it; and have dominion over the fish of the sea and over the birds of the air and over every living thing that moves upon the earth. (Gen.1. 27–28).

This 'ideal state' disintegrated with the Fall when dominance, subservience, roles based on gender rather than equality of gifting, and stereotyping came into the picture. When St Paul says in Gal.3.28, 'There is no longer Jew or Greek, there is no longer slave or free, there is no longer male and female; for all of you are one in

Christ Jesus', he is alluding to the work of redemption brought in with the death and Resurrection of Christ. It is a work of redemption that will one day be achieved in full with the return of Christ. The vision for the new heaven and the new earth is one in which all prejudice, injustice, sin, stereotype – in fact all the consequences of sin and the Fall – will be redeemed; when the coming kingdom has come in its completeness.

As Christians we join in with continuing to bring in that redemption which was won by Christ's death on the Cross. We too can help in God's 'forward-looking' work of restoring all of creation. One of the places we can begin this prophetic work is in the everyday experience of juggling between men and women, work and home, pointing forward to God's intended reclamation of the perfect harmony that existed before the Fall, in the relationships between people, men and women, and with the whole of creation.

We need to recapture that sense of 'doing all of it together'. So every time a man and a woman work constructively together as colleagues, every time a man and a woman communicate together about how they might best *both* fulfil their vocations, every time a man and a woman commit to working together to raise a family, every time a man and a woman share in the tasks of the home, every time a man and a woman share in the leading of a church, every time a woman and a man are friends, every time a man and a woman release each other into doing what they are made to do, then the kingdom comes a little more.

Sacrifice

The question needs to be asked whether we are trying to have it all, or simply to have it all at once. I believe that it is possible for women and for men to enjoy a career, a marriage, a family, a faith and a fulfilled social life, but that, at times, something has to give in order to let other things thrive.

For some people that might mean part-time work when children are small and more chance to reach the top as they grow older. It might mean two parents working part-time and sharing childcare. It might mean giving less time to church activities if you work full-time. It might mean the cleaning doesn't get done every week. It will almost certainly mean a lower standard of living than might have been achievable if you did have it all, all at once. Above all, it will involve sacrifice.

Sacrifice is not a popular concept at the moment. You're not meant to give things up. You're meant to take it all. I was in the cinema with my family the other day and two of the adverts shown before the film started struck me. One of them was for a children's TV channel and its strapline was 'It's all about you'. Another ad, for a satellite TV network, promised, 'Entertainment your way'. These two media companies are not alone in marketing themselves on the assumption that everyone puts themselves first. It is my choices that matter. I'm the important one. I should be able to have whatever I want. It's my right and if I don't get it, someone else is to blame.

That is very different from the Christian way; the way of the cross, where the first shall be last and the last first, where you go the extra mile, where you consider others more than yourself.

If a Christian way of living is one of consideration and respect, which places the needs of the other person as equally as important as, if not more important than, my own needs, sacrifice is the next step. Sacrifice is the act or attitude of giving yourself up for the good of another person, or giving up something you would like to do or have for the benefit of another. It is 'forfeiture of something highly valued for the sake of one considered to have a greater value or claim'. In reality, much of our relating with other people needs to involve an element of sacrifice for it to work at all.

We see sacrifice around us all the time in many different forms, not all of them applauded and recognized: the mother who works part-time and therefore sacrifices her 'right' to the same salary as a man who does not. The man who sacrifices his old life 'out with the lads' every night in order to put his kids to bed. The couple who sacrifice their 'right' to live in a town of their choosing, to be near elderly parents who need caring for. All over the place people are making sacrifices for people they love, and yet it is not a concept that has much regard in popular culture.

Sacrifice – for another person, for a better way of living, for God, who knows all about sacrifice anyway – is at the heart of the Christian faith. Jesus laid down all the riches of heaven for the love of humanity when he was born as a baby. He was offered the chance to 'have it all' in the desert by the devil and he turned it down. Ultimately, he sacrificed his life on the Cross.

Is it possible to have it all? Not if you also want to have healthy and fulfilled relationships with those around you. In looking at the busyness of your life there may be things you have to sacrifice, for the sake of others – a bigger house in the right area for the sake of spending more time with your family and less time at work, a career promotion for the sake of your sanity, something you might have done for something your partner wants to do and so on. Sacrifice is never easy, but it is good news. Why?

Sacrifice of this type for another is the way of freedom. Discerning what you should be doing, in a spirit of sacrificial love, and living in that alone brings great liberty. It is life as God intended. It is fasting as well as feasting. At the end of the day it is about being brave and making realistic choices – deciding what is really important, what God is calling you to do and going for it with all the energy, enthusiasm and confidence you have in your being, alongside those with whom God has called you to live your life.

A godly perspective

Jesus didn't promise that we would have it all. Quite the contrary. He talked about making sacrifices and laying down your life for your friends. However, he did promise us a full and varied life.

Christians have sometimes been afraid of taking Jesus up on this promise. We have fretted over our busyness, worried about doing too much, but not done much about it. Perhaps we have also used talk of 'being too busy' as an excuse for not embracing all that God has in store for us. If you can't have it all, you need to be able to make the right, godly, choices according to priorities and vocation. What are *you* called by God to do at this time? And what are you called not to do?

Jesus calls us to high standards. The commandment that 'You shall love the Lord your God with all your heart, and with all your soul, and with all your strength, and with all your mind; and your neighbour as yourself' (Lk. 10.27) is not really something that can be done in half measures. Jesus himself was someone about whom it was said, 'He has done everything well' (Mk. 7.37). There is an impulse in many of us to do things well too. The trouble is there is an instinct literally to do *everything* well, which is just not possible. Jesus does not call us to be stressed and stretched. He did say, 'My burden is easy and my yoke is light' (Mt. 11.40). It is possible to find this lightness in the busyness, to experience the 'burden' of living as easy. But only if we redeem busyness, and claim it as part of God's plan, not contrary to it.

Stepping above

Organize your life! That's the solution most often offered to help us get a handle on the busyness. 'Just get organized,' we think, 'and it will be OK.' The answer is not more time-management, as if all we needed to do to become less busy was to organize what we have to do better. Time- and stress-management principles are helpful, but they often mean we treat the symptoms rather than the real problem. If it doesn't fit, it doesn't fit. The answer is not to re-arrange it but to reassess it; to ask the bigger questions about what we're doing and why.

If we're too busy, our real need isn't to learn how to squeeze more into our lives – to live more efficiently – but to refocus our lives on what matters most: to live more effectively and therefore to make choices. But it's hard to find the time and the space to do that in everyday life. 'Sorting my life out' or 'deciding what to do and what not to do' gets put to the bottom of the 'To do' list because it's hard work. It takes time, energy and soul-searching. We know thinking about it might be painful, and we might have to make some changes as a result. And so we put it off. We're too busy to think about how we might make choices to help us not to be too busy. This book is intended to provide the 'space' or motivation you need to begin to make some of those choices.

When I was very busy at Lee Abbey, I would often climb a hill above the Lee Abbey buildings. From the top of the hill where it was still and quiet, I could look down at my life (or at least the place I lived it) from above. I could still hear the sounds of life going on below me. I could usually hear my four-year-old (he has that kind of voice). But I was above it all, peaceful and unreachable. Up there I had space and stillness and I would reflect and pray about all I had to do. Somehow that physical act of 'stepping above' gave me a new viewpoint. It helped me to regain a sense of calm and order and to hear God's voice above the clamour. I felt equipped after my times on the top of the hill to go down and live my life again with a fresh perspective.

This book could function as your hillside vantage point. It is intended to give you some of that 'above' time, a chance to examine what life holds for you, and how to make a difference to it in partnership with those with whom you share it. It is a chance to rise above the busyness and ask some searching questions of the messages coming at you from the world below you. In discerning the different voices that you hear – from your culture, from your church, from your family and friends, from yourself – you will be better able to prioritize your times and your energy and to find God's still, small voice in the midst of it all. It is a chance to ask some probing questions of yourself, your vocation and your life choices. The hope is that in finding God's calling on each of our lives, we will find ourselves too.

By the way, this book is a guilt-free zone. A lot of people are busy, but feel guilty about what they are not doing, or not doing enough of. This book is designed to help you to work out what to do and to do it fully, without guilt.

Live life to the full. Do more, not less. And enjoy it.

Having time

2

Why are we so busy?

If I were to phone my friends and family today and ask them how they are, I guarantee that one word will surface more than most: busy. This is how the conversation would go. Me: 'How are you?' My friend: 'Oh, fine. Busy.' Being busy is the state that comes to mind more readily than being well or happy or sad or fulfilled or frustrated. Being busy is our modern condition. If you are not busy, you must be doing something wrong.

You have only to do a cursory search of the Internet to find thousands of websites aimed at helping busy people to be less stressed, more organized and, well, less busy. There is a plethora of 'biblical' material aimed at helping busy Christians. Most of it describes busyness as something Christians should avoid if they are to have any hope of getting close to God. Various articles speak of 'busy sickness', the 'plague of busyness', 'the tyranny of busyness' and 'the disease of busyness'. I have found features devoted to helping me to 'say no to busyness' and even to 'resist the demon of busyness'. Much of it suggests that if we all stopped being so busy everything would be all right, we would regain order in our lives, God's mission would be advanced, the Church would be revived and world peace would break out.

But is that true?

It's a big question and in order to begin to answer it we have to ask some other questions first. There are three that arise. The first is: what is busyness anyway? The second follows on from the first: why are we so busy? The third is this: is it OK to be busy, or is busyness something to be avoided at all costs, especially by Christians who seek to do the will of God?

What is busyness?

So first of all let us ask, what is busyness?

The word itself seems to have become accepted parlance only recently. Before about ten years ago, you couldn't speak very easily of 'busyness'. There was no such word. You could speak of 'being busy', but if you tried to make it into a noun and spell it, it came out too much like 'business' which is something else altogether. Recently, however, 'busyness' has become a more acceptable word. Perhaps that's because busyness has become a more acceptable state. I'll explain what I mean by that in a minute.

But first – definitions. Dictionary definitions point to busyness being about lots of activity. The *Oxford English Dictionary* defines being busy as 'having a great deal to do',[1] *Collins English Dictionary* as 'actively or fully engaged; occupied; crowded with or characterized by activity'.[2] Incidentally, you can only look up 'busy'. Neither dictionary has a separate entry for the word 'busyness'.

It is all very well to define busyness, but we need to remember that 'being busy' is a state of mind rather than a state of affairs. Busyness is about perception of oneself and the tasks one has to complete in a set time: 'Busyness is a subjective state, which results from the individual's assessment of her or his own recent or expected activity patterns, in the light of current norms and expectations.'[3] What one person might consider as incredibly busy might be, for someone else, having an easy time of it. We all have slightly different perceptions of what 'busy' means and problems arise when we try to communicate with each other about what it feels like. I spoke to someone the other day who described herself as busy. Probing a little further into what that meant, she outlined a plan for her week that for me would have been a walk in the park! She thought she was busy because she had *one* thing to do each

---

1. *Oxford English Dictionary* (Oxford University Press, 2005).
2. *Collins English Dictionary* (Collins, 2006).
3. Jonathan Gershuny, 'Busyness as the badge of honour for the new superordinate working class', Working Papers of the Institute for Social and Economic Research, paper 2005–6, Colchester: University of Essex (2005), p. 16.

day! 'You think *you're* busy,' I thought to myself. 'You should try living *my* life!' Yet she felt herself to be busy.

There might be a tendency for people to use the glib phrase 'I'm too busy' to resist doing something they have been asked to do, or to avoid taking on a task. That causes stress and irritation in the person doing the asking if their perception is that the person's busyness is small-fry.

Added to this is the fact that there are different kinds of busyness. The first kind of busyness is simply having a lot to fill our day, being active and enjoying it, working, doing, caring, laughing, walking, driving, being. That kind of busyness leaves us full of the joys of spring.

Then there are those times that are busier than others. The time before a major event at work, the time around major exams, the early years with pre-school children, the time just before Christmas. If you know these very busy times are finite and for a season, you can cope with that kind of busyness.

There is a third kind of busyness – the relentless, draining busyness that carries on and on, when life simply holds too much, and you know you are not coping any more. This is a feeling that what you have on your plate is simply too much for anyone to handle, when the tasks you have to achieve each day simply do not fit into the time allocated and you know you can't go on at that pace. It's when you find yourself thinking, 'This used to be fine, but now it doesn't fit. I'm not making the choices any more, this thing is driving me, rather than the other way around.' It's the feeling that you're juggling lots of balls and sooner or later you're going to drop one. You carry on being too busy, thinking it will end soon, even when it's not showing any signs of abating. 'This is just a busy phase,' you say to yourself. 'Things will calm down soon.' And they never do.

So how do we learn to live mostly in type one busyness, where busyness is something that is good and energizing and feels like really living? It may be simply a matter of attitude change. Rather than thinking, 'I'm constantly busy and it's a problem', maybe we need to start thinking, 'I am busy. That's a fact. Now how do I make sure I'm busy doing the right things – and how might I begin to enjoy it?'

What is required may be more than a simple change in thinking, though. Sometimes radical changes in lifestyle and choices may be needed in addition.

So there are different perceptions of busyness and different types of busyness. Allowing for all that, the general agreement seems to be that we are getting busier, or at least perceiving ourselves to be. Why is that?

Messages: Why are we so busy?

Being busy is all about time, and time is something we're very interested in these days. A recent study found that 'time' is the most commonly used noun in the English language (the nouns 'day' and 'week' also came in the top ten). We talk about time a lot, which is not surprising because some might say we're obsessed with time and with what we do with it.

Time-management consultancy is a burgeoning industry. Time has become a precious commodity, and like stocks and shares and investment accounts there are plenty of people around who can tell us how to manage it better, in order to reap the highest returns. People speak of being 'time poor'. Our perception of time and the way we 'spend' (note the language of economics) it is the key thing.

The reason many of us are so concerned with time is that often we don't think we have enough of it. We perceive that we have too much to do and too little time in which to do it. For many people who live and work in the western world today there is simply so much that *could* be done. Whilst the tasks to be accomplished have expanded and increased, whether at home, at work, in church or wherever, the time we have to do them in has not. An hour still has 60 minutes in it, a day still consists of 24 hours and a week still has seven days. There are still 365 and a quarter days in a year. So time stays the same, activities increase. Something doesn't add up any more. It is a basic economy.

How has this state of affairs come about? There are many reasons why we should have *more* time on our hands than our mothers and fathers did. Household appliances such as washing machines, vacuum cleaners, dishwashers, tumble driers and bread makers mean we have to spend less time caring for our homes and families. Cars are more reliable, go faster and more of us own them so we don't have to spend as much time getting from A to B. At work, gadgets like BlackBerries, laptops and mobile phones mean we can work anywhere, and work-smart practices aim to increase the amount we can achieve in any set time. You can even have your shopping delivered to your door. So why are we so busy, when we're meant to be so much better at squeezing what we do into the time we have? There ought to be more time, not less.

The crux is this: although doing things takes less time, we're doing more of them. Life today offers vast opportunities, for both men and women, but it also brings stern demands. Cars are faster and more reliable, but we travel further to work. Mobile phones mean we can work from anywhere we like, but also mean we can be contacted whenever anyone else likes. There has been a raising of expectations about the amount of different occupations it is possible for one person to be engaged in at any one time.

Christians today, especially perhaps professionals, particularly maybe those raised in the 'have it all era' of the 1980s and 1990s, have set the standards very high. We worked very hard for our degrees and our qualifications and we continue to strive to achieve our full potential in our chosen field of work. Those of us who are married went to marriage preparation sessions first. We know all the theory about what makes for good and sustainable relationships and so we invest time and energy in our marriages – and we're not afraid to talk about sex. Many couples now genuinely seek to be the best parents possible, have been on parenting courses and know that quality (and quantity) time is important in raising healthy, balanced children. We buy books about bringing up children successfully. We might even have found time to read them. We know about healthy diet and exercise. We join the gym. We read magazines that help us to lead a more active life-style. We are paying a fortune to service our mortgages and we want our homes to look nice too. We admire Nigella Lawson and Cath Kidston. We leave copies of *Country Living* lying about on our coffee tables.

Partnership and sacrifice

Whereas my mother's generation would never have dreamt of even attempting to do as much as we do, today's world has been designed to encourage us to try. In those days, you devoted yourself primarily to one thing. You chose between having a family and having a career. For most men it was work that occupied their time – and family life fitted around it. For most women it was family and home life, and work fitted around it (and then only if you had to work). Today, many women have careers as well as families and more and more men are taking seriously the responsibility of family life. Our society demands that both sexes do more than ever before and that we do them better. And so we place greater and greater expectations upon ourselves.

This is true particularly of women. We are still proving ourselves in the big wide world of the workplace. Alongside this has been the burgeoning of post-feminism. We have rediscovered the importance of mothering and the lost arts of child-rearing and homemaking. So now we try to do *both* well: 'It used to be enough to be a good businesswoman. Now we feel we have to be a good businesswoman and a mother, and a wife, and wear the right shoes. And being women, we think that by trying harder, better, in stereo, we'll make things improve.'[4]

There are some good motives behind this pressure towards excellence. Many of us rejoice that the days are long gone when a woman was expected simply to care for her children and home and that was it. Some women were, and are, happy with pursuing this single calling, but there are others of us who know that our vocation includes work outside the home too. At last society has begun to utilize the gifts and potential of women in all areas of public life. I am delighted to see the increasing number of men who now know that fatherhood is as much a calling as their paid work is, and who strive to spend time with their families. Parenting has become a matter for serious research and professionalism.

4. Bedell, 'What makes women happy?'.

Taking care of a home has also become an important and ful-filling business. More and more people are putting huge amounts of time and effort (and money) into the decoration, design and maintenance of their homes and gardens. We know so much more about health and fitness now, and recognize the importance of getting regular exercise and maintaining a healthy lifestyle, which can only be a good thing.

The Church is increasingly aware of the fact that it is viewed by the rest of society as unattractive, shabby and amateurish. For too long church has been shoddy and Christians seen as slightly less than normal. There is a growing realization that if the Church in Britain is going to make any impact for the gospel on the lives of ordinary men and women, it is going to have to do things more professionally. Our sights have been rightly raised to think about fresh expressions of church, and new ways of being church, and mission-shaped church and café church and liquid church, and so on. It seems to me that the Church as a whole is rejoicing in a new-found confidence and hope for the future. But it takes a lot of commitment (and lots of meetings) to get it right. Perfection is unattainable, but excellence, we now know, is not.

Then there are our own personal lives with God. There's so much available to help us now: books and courses and programmes all designed to make sure that we spend every minute of our purpose-driven, mission-shaped, spirit-filled day with Jesus.

I do believe God wants us to set the highest standards for ourselves and for others as we seek him with all our hearts. All these ambitions and expectations are good and laudable. But all of them together have a tendency to lead us to become over-busy and burnt out.

There are also very many negative motivations for busyness too – the need to own more, the push for more money and influence and power, the need to be seen to be successful, the desire to be liked by everyone, the drive to impress, the compulsion to achieve physical perfection, the tendency to find identity in what one does (no less so in the Church) rather than who one is. All of these things too can drive us, Christians included, to ever-increasing busyness.

There is another more subtle change going on too. It has become more acceptable, and desirable, to *be seen* as busy. It has become trendy to be busy. In Victorian society, if you were wealthy and successful, you were not busy. Wealth enabled you to employ people to be busy for you. The seriously wealthy never worked, but employed servants to do the menial tasks for them. They were known as the 'leisured' classes for a reason. Today, that is very different. Of the top 1,000 wealthiest people in Britain today, 750 are self-made millionaires who made their money in land, property, banking or finance. It has not landed in their lap. They have not inherited it. They have earned it by being busy. And so busyness has come to be equated with wealth and success. The subliminal message we receive all the time is this: busy people are successful. In today's culture, one of the things that marks you out as significant and a valuable contributor to your society/ business/workplace/family/church is the fact that you are busy. Busyness has become the new badge of honour.

So, many people are busy. Many people enjoy being busy. Many people don't want to be quite so busy. Some people enjoy complaining about being busy. How do we know whether our motivations towards increasing activity are good or bad? What would God say about our busyness? Where is God in it all?

Is it OK to be busy?

If we look again at the dictionary definitions we saw earlier, busyness is about being active, not about being *too* active. Being busy is simply being occupied, having things to do. What scares us is when now and again it becomes too much.

This struck me dramatically one day recently when I was doing some photocopying. I do not usually have life-changing moments when photocopying, but this day I did. I knew I had a certain number of copies to do, and that they had to be done *now*. I knew also that I had to leave to pick my daughter up from school at 3.20. It was 3.10. I found myself timing how long each copy took to emerge from the copier, and counting how many copies I had left, and dividing one figure by the other in order to work out whether I would have enough time to complete the photocopying or not.

My life had become so busy that the preciousness of my time was measured by the few seconds it took to produce one photocopy. It was at that point that I knew that I was too busy and that something had to go.

By the way, in case you're wondering, I did make it to pick my daughter up and the photocopying didn't get finished. Surprisingly, the world didn't fall apart.

A Godly perspective

A biblical perspective on busyness

Christianity can be seen as a busy religion. Christianity has a strong contemplative tradition, so we may find it surprising when it is seen by others to be a religion in a rush. The main character in the Booker Prize-winning novel *Life of Pi* is born a Hindu and sees Christianity in this way:

> Christianity is a religion in a rush. Look at the world created in seven days. Even at a symbolic level, that's creation at a frenzy. ... If Hinduism flows placidly like the Ganges, Christianity bustles like Toronto at rush hour. It is a religion as swift as a swallow, as urgent as an ambulance. In a moment, you are lost or saved. Christianity stretches back through the ages, but in essence it exists only at one time: right now.[5]

We may want to question some of Pi's assumptions about the Christian faith, and yet it rings true.

Is God busy? It's a question you don't often hear asked, but if we are wondering whether an active and busy life is best for our well-being, is God busy and active too? I know there are many senses in which we would not want, or indeed be able, to act as God does. We are not omnipotent, omnipresent and omniscient for a start.

5. Yann Martel, *Life of Pi* (Canongate Books, 2003).

But there may be aspects of God's activity that we would want to learn from.

Is God busy?

Being God must, in itself, be a very busy task. Throughout the Bible we see God being active and, you might say, busy. God is an energetic, creative God.

God made the world in six days (or, as the Hebrew would have it, six periods of time). God had a plan for making the universe and he worked until he had achieved it. At the end of that time, God rested: a pattern of work and rest that we shall explore in Chapter 9. But God didn't stop work when he'd made the universe. He's carried on ever since. The Scriptures paint the picture of a God who is so concerned, obsessed even, with building a relationship with humankind, that he works day and night to create, nurture, warn, reprimand, console, cajole, encourage, bless, defend, support and love his people.

God ordained that life should consist of day and night, work and rest and yet the Psalms speak of God as so concerned to protect his people that he does not even risk sleep: 'He will not let your foot be moved; he who keeps you will not slumber. He who keeps Israel will neither slumber nor sleep' (Ps. 121.3–4). When Jesus is questioned by the religious leaders about his healing of a man on the Sabbath he says to them: 'My Father is still working, and I also am working' (Jn 5.17). The picture is of a dynamic God reflected in the dynamic work of his Son.

God and time

We have seen that time is one of the most precious commodities we have. Yet God has an eternal perspective on time from which we can learn. God specializes in bringing order out of chaos. One of the ways in which he does this is instilling in his creation an innate sense of time.

God has created and maintains a natural cycle of days, weeks, months. The biblical view is that God is in control of time and has given human beings an innate sense of rhythm and pace. From the very beginning when God said, 'Let there be lights in the dome of the sky to separate the day from the night; and let them be for signs and for seasons and for days and years' (Gen. 1.14), the whole of creation has had an inbuilt sense of season, rhythm and time pattern ordained by its creator: 'Yours is the day, yours also the night; you established the luminaries and the sun. You have fixed all the bounds of the earth; you made summer and winter' (Ps. 74.16–17). This state of affairs is to endure always: 'As long as the earth endures, seedtime and harvest, cold and heat, summer and winter, day and night, shall not cease' (Gen. 8.22). God orders time for the good of his creation and human beings are designed to respect and respond to this sense of ordered time: 'I have seen the business that God has given to everyone to be busy with. He has made everything suitable for its time; moreover, he has put a sense of past and future into their minds' (Eccl. 3.9–11).

Our bodies are designed for periods of wakefulness and periods of sleep, and our health suffers if we have too much of one or the other. The human body is hardwired to respond to changes of light and darkness in a 24-hour period. Research has shown that working too much at night is bad for your health. One recent study found a link between exposure to light at night and the suppression of the body's physiological production of melatonin, a hormone that protects against certain intestinal cancers. We function best if we include in our lives times of activity and times of rest. Our bodies, especially those of women, are also made to respond to and reflect the lunar, monthly cycle.

God's desire is that we order our time well and in accordance with the created order he has put in place, so that life will go well for us. Not to do so is to risk our health, physical, emotional and spiritual. God's intention is that, like him, we should be in control of time, not controlled by it, that we should be conscious in the decisions we make about the way we will spend our time, 'redeeming' it (Col. 4.5) and using it wisely.

That's easier said than done! It's all very well for God, we might say. God is God. He doesn't have my pressures and stresses. He doesn't know what it is like to be human. In fact, he does.

Jesus was busy

In Jesus God has lived amongst us and shared our joys, our sorrows and our time pressures. What was Jesus's attitude to time? Like his Father, he was very busy. He had a mission to fulfil and a short time in which to do it. He lived only 33 years. He was only in public ministry for three years and he was under constant pressure. He was pursued by the crowds, by his followers, by his enemies: '. . . the crowds were looking for him; and when they reached him, they wanted to prevent him from leaving them' (Lk. 4.42).

In Mark 1, as Jesus heals Simon's mother-in-law the whole town gather round the door to watch. No sooner does he retreat for a bit of peace and quiet, than Simon comes looking for him – hunting for him: 'Everyone is searching for you' (Mk 1.37). The Gospel of Mark is an urgent gospel. It is full of words like 'immediately' and 'at once'. You might call it 'the busy gospel'.

Jesus was very busy. And yet he had a clear sense of what he was on earth to do, having set out his 'mission statement' in Lk. 4.18: 'The spirit of the Lord is upon me, because he has anointed me to preach good news to the poor. He has sent me to proclaim freedom for the prisoners and recovery of sight for the blind, to release the oppressed, to proclaim the year of the Lord's favour.' That was his mission – a busy and demanding one – and he allocated his time according to it. He did lots of things while he was on earth, but all of his activity was consistent with God's plan and purpose. He made choices based on those plans and purposes.

Sometimes his choices surprised people. In Luke 18, Jesus is on his final walk into Jerusalem, approaching the city in which he will be crucified. He comes to Jericho, just a short step from his final destination. As he goes into the town, he hears a voice, 'Jesus, Son of David, have mercy on me!', and he stops, much to the annoyance of his disciples who see his stopping as a diversion – and not part of their plan. Doesn't Jesus appreciate that Jerusalem is six hours' walk away? They would like to get there in time for the Passover. His friends would have the right to be irritated, if the only purpose of Jesus's life was to reach the city in time for the religious celebration. But Jesus knows that his mission is to touch broken people. And so he stops and heals the blind man. He adds an extra activity to his already busy schedule, but the choice to do so comes out of an overarching knowledge of what his mission and purpose is. So it is the right choice, rather than an extra pressure on an already busy man[6].

Worried and upset: the story of Martha and Mary

One of my favourite stories in the Gospels is the occasion where Jesus goes to visit his dear friends, the sisters Mary and Martha (Lk. 10.38–42)[7]. Mary and Martha are often held up as opposites. Mary is the calm, serene, holy one who 'spends time with Jesus' at his feet. And Martha is the flustered one, who is distracted and unholy. Mary equals the spiritual. Martha equals the human. Mary equals sorted. Martha equals stressed. Above all, Martha is held up as the abject lesson in why we should not allow ourselves to get too busy.

Is that really what is going on in this story? Let's take another look.

Jesus and his followers are travelling towards Jerusalem. They come to a 'certain village' and there they are welcomed by Martha into her home. Martha's gift to Jesus is her welcome, her hospitality. In Middle Eastern culture, hospitality was very important and not to have provided a meal for the guests would have been considered extremely rude, unthinkable even. Someone had to prepare it and that someone was Martha. In offering hospitality to Jesus, being busy in the kitchen, Martha is not sinning, she is not 'going against God's will for her life'; she is simply getting on with what is expected and good and necessary – and busy.

Jesus never condemns Martha's busyness *per se*. Being busy is not the problem. In other places Jesus praises 'doing' and busyness. In

---

6. See Gordon MacDonald, *Ordering Your Private World* (Highland Books, 1987) for further reading on how Jesus spent his time.
7. I am grateful to the insights of the Revd Jackie Searle on this passage.

one story of the talents, the high achiever gets the rewards, and the laid-back lazy one gets called 'wicked'. And we have already seen that Jesus himself was busy, much of the time.

While Martha busies herself in the kitchen, Mary listens to Jesus's teaching. Many people think of Mary as the model of a submissive, subservient woman, sitting at Jesus's feet, gracefully taking in all he says. She probably has a slight glow round her head. But Mary is doing something totally shocking and unacceptable. She is making a bold and radical statement in sitting at Jesus's feet. In those days, the way you showed you were a disciple of your chosen rabbi was to sit at his feet as he taught. That way, you showed that you wanted to be a disciple – in order to become a rabbi yourself. Mary is behaving as if she were a man! No respectable rabbi would let a woman learn from him. But Jesus lets her sit at his feet and commends her outrageous behaviour: 'Mary has chosen the better thing: only one thing is needed.'

The 'one thing' is not staring at her navel all her life, sitting in quiet contemplation, resisting busyness at all costs. It is, rather, being 'at the feet of Jesus', being his follower, his disciple, following her own calling to be a rabbi. 'That's the most important thing,' Jesus says. 'Follow me, whatever you're doing, whether you're really busy or not. Be my disciple.'

What Jesus challenges Martha for is not being busy, but being 'worried and upset about many things'. The word used means 'pulled apart'. Some translations say 'distracted'. Jesus does not condemn any of us for being busy. I believe it is his intention that we should live our lives to the full, being active, stretching, choosing, risking, doing, changing the world. It is when we become 'worried and upset' by the tasks we have included in our lives that we need to stop and look again at our choices, with God's help.

The 'yes' God

Busy Christians are often being told that they just need to learn to say 'no'. I have lost count of the number of times I have been told this. I know people say it out of a sense of concern for me and wanting to 'rescue' me from my perpetually busy state, but if I'm honest, it has started to irritate me. Saying 'no' seems to have become the ultimate tool for success as a Christian. If you learn to say 'no' properly, then you've really made it.

The trouble is, I don't really want to be a person who says 'no'. I want to be a person who says 'yes' – to God, to other people, to life. I believe in a God who has said an almighty and resounding 'yes' to humankind in his work of redemption through Jesus. He is an overwhelmingly, outrageously generous and giving God. Everything about the God I love screams 'YES!' Perhaps we need to learn to say 'yes' more. Not 'yes' to every demand and request that comes our way, but 'yes' to the requests that fit in with God's plans, reflecting the nature of our generous, open, giving God in everything we do.

Jesus went through his life saying 'yes' to people. He said 'no' very rarely. In fact, Jesus's whole life was one big 'yes' – a busy, active, can-do 'yes' to every person he met and in the Cross and Resurrection, to the whole of humankind. If we follow him we will be 'yes' people, active in the world, fulfilling God's mission and advancing his kingdom on earth.

Stepping above

The question still remains – how do we do this without becoming stressed and burnt out, without becoming 'worried and upset'?

Doing too much can lead to our feeling like we can't do anything well. St Vincent de Paul, writing in the seventeenth century said: '[Busyness] is a trick of the Devil, which he employs to deceive good souls to incite them to do more than they are able, in order that they may no longer be able to do anything.' When we know that we are doing 'more than we are able', that's when we need to make choices about what we can do and what we simply cannot do. The answer is to ask the bigger questions about what you are doing and why, to have a 'mission', as Jesus did, and to live by it. Then, like Jesus, we will know what our calling is and therefore say 'yes' to the things that God wants us to (and 'no' to the things he doesn't).

Psalm 90 talks about the fleeting nature of our lives. The prayer of the Psalmist is that God would teach us to 'count our days that we may gain a wise heart' (Ps. 90.12). As you read this book and reflect on your own life, that is my prayer for you too.

Occupation

3

Work as blessing not burden

Work: 'This is what we do'

Work is part of God's good plan for his people. It is a basic human
activity – whether it is going to work in an office, school, hospital,
or caring for livestock or growing produce, doing voluntary care
work in the community, studying, looking after children and
home, working full-time, part-time or hourly, being paid or
unpaid, work is what we do with our waking hours, and it is a
fundamental part of our existence.

An important point to be made right at the start is that work is
not only what you are paid for. There are many people today
working very hard and not getting paid a penny – parents working
in the tasks of the home, voluntary workers in the community,
faithful saints serving the Church in ways that are not paid. As Paul
wrote: 'Whatever you do, in word or deed, do everything in the
name of the Lord Jesus, giving thanks to God the Father through
him' (Col. 3.17). Your work is 'whatever you do' day by day.

At a very basic level, work is the way a society maintains itself
and provides the goods and services it needs. The parent looking
after children at home is 'providing' to society the benefit of
bringing up well-adjusted smaller members of that society. The
volunteer worker provides without pay the care or services needed
by society. The student provides for society by training in skills
that will benefit others.

Although work can be paid or unpaid, the way we work and
what we get paid for it has an enormous effect on the way we view
ourselves and our worth. I have always had a dubious relationship

with salary. For many years I was a student, studying for a masters and then a doctoral degree. For some of that time Mat had a good job and supported me in my study. I got used to many comments from people about my being a 'kept woman'. Then I worked at home looking after our daughter when she was very young. It wasn't paid at all, yet it was the hardest and most demanding job I have ever done. When we were curates, the diocese refused to split a stipend and declared that only one of us would be paid. The other had to be 'non-stipendiary'. In order to overturn possible presuppositions about who would be the unpaid one, I got the stipend and Mat didn't. We didn't tell many people, for fear that Mat's ministry would be looked down upon because he did it for free. At Lee Abbey we didn't get paid, but got a living allowance that went to our family as a whole, rather than being attached to the specific chaplaincy work that we were doing. At one point of particular stress on our household, I suddenly realized that it would be perfectly possible for me to give up working altogether without it affecting our family income. I didn't, but again it made us think about the nature of the work we were doing. On leaving Lee Abbey we have decided that only Mat should look for paid work. While we settle in as a family, and while I write this book, I'm not doing a job I'm paid for. I do some work for an organization locally once a week, but that organization can't afford to pay me so I do it for free. I am busier than ever, getting used to a new church and community, doing voluntary work, writing and speaking engagements. Yet I don't see a penny for it.

This raises mixed feelings in me. On the one hand I believe God has called me to live in this way at this time, and I value being able to be free to take my children to school and pick them up, for example. But I have been surprised at how much it matters to me that I am doing all this for no money. It has affected the way I view my work and the way I see myself. I have asked questions about whether I am worth being paid. I have got frustrated at minor tasks because I am seeing no financial reward. We are not flushed with cash at the moment, and there is guilt that I am not helping Mat to provide for our family in financial terms. Not being paid for a job does affect the way you see that job, your self-esteem and feeling of being valued by the organization you work for, and the motivation to work hard. I am realizing that it was with insight that Paul writes to Timothy: 'the labourer deserves to be paid' (1 Tim. 5.18). However, Jesus calls people to offer their work for the kingdom in a way that does not expect financial reward: 'Cure the sick, raise the dead, cleanse the lepers, cast out demons. You received without payment; give without payment' (Mt. 10.8).

The key factor in all of this is vocation. If God is calling you to work without pay, whether it be in the voluntary sector or at home or as a student or out of the good of your heart, that is your ministry and your mission for this time and its value should not be underestimated, by yourself or anyone else.

For many people the world of work is a pleasure: it is where they are able to use their skills, qualities and characteristics; it is where they are able to make a contribution to their families and to society; it is often where they gain a sense of self-worth and value. The trouble is that work also has the potential to be the greatest source of stress and anxiety – the unemployed middle-aged person who sees no prospect of getting another paid job; those trapped in repetitive, exploitative work for low pay; the executives who spend far too much of their week in the office or travelling to it, but who are afraid to cut their hours for fear of what it might suggest to the boss; the father at home who finds the task of caring for a small, demanding child depressing and isolating; the working mother who feels guilty about leaving her children, as well as guilty about leaving the office early to get home for them; the older people who work well into their advancing years, not because they want to, but because they need to increase a meagre pension.

The Bible sees work as having a godly imperative, as if we are serving him: 'Whatever your task, put yourselves into it, as done for the Lord and not for your masters, since you know that from the Lord you will receive the inheritance as your reward; you serve the Lord Christ' (Col. 4.22–24). However, the temptation has often been to see work as simply 'that thing that I do', not on a Sunday and therefore outside the remit of God's grace. Nothing could be further from the truth.

Many Christians have never been encouraged to take the 'above' perspective on their working lives and to ask questions about calling and priorities. Mark Greene of the London Institute for Contemporary Christianity laments the fact that 50 per cent of people in one study had never heard a sermon on work, 75 per cent have never heard anyone suggest a theology of work and only 25 per cent have been encouraged to see what they do at work as ministry.

It is all the more important at this time that Christians see work as a fully integrated part of their walk with God and have something to say about work to the people around them, because now, more than ever, the world of work is in crisis. Mark Greene says: 'Today – in the West at least – it is not the physical conditions of work that we need to battle, it is the psychological conditions of work. The crisis is this: how can we flourish economically and still have lives worth living?'[1] The pressure to work longer and longer hours, the drive for higher salaries to meet escalating housing costs and several other factors lead to a culture where work has become the be all and end all of life, and the rest – family, friendships, social lives and health – has to fit in around the edges. It is a situation that is affecting relationships, health and well-being and that, for many, is not sustainable in the long term.

Messages

The long hours culture

Advances have been made in the way we work and the machines we have available to help us. People used to predict that working hours would get shorter as a result. Juliet Schor claims that if we were to accept living standards similar to those enjoyed by the average middle-class person in the 1950s, these advancements should have made a full-time working day a mere four hours long.[2] The reality for many is very different. Work has got busier and the hours have got longer, not shorter.

---

1. Mark Greene, 'Slave new world', at www.LICC.org.uk.
2. Juliet Schor, *The Overworked American: The unexpected decline of leisure*, cited in Suzanne Franks, *Having None of It* (Granta Books, 2000), p. 68.

The average hours worked by British workers are 43.6 per week. In the rest of the EU the average is 40.3.[3] Only 44 per cent of workers in Britain use their full holiday entitlement. The reasons they give for not taking all their holiday are heavy workload and fear of upsetting the boss; 65 per cent do not take a lunch break.[4]

This week I saw the current leader of the Liberal Democrats, Menzies Campbell, interviewed on television. The interviewer put to him the accusation that he was too old to lead his party to power. He retorted: 'I'm up to the job. I'm still very energetic. Yesterday I did an 18-hour day.' For Campbell the proof that he was worth his keep as party leader was that he could work for 18 hours out of 24. He wore his long hours with pride. When the President of the United Sates of America, George Bush, admitted that he likes to go to bed early and work short hours, his commitment to the task was questioned: 'Going to bed whenever you want is one of the great benefits of adulthood, and anyone who uses that freedom to retire at 7.45 is to be regarded with suspicion. If Bush wants to keep farmer's hours, that is his business, but it does confirm the popular view of him as a man insufficiently preoccupied by the cares of office.'[5] How has it come to this, when the ability to work ridiculous hours is lauded and the desire to get a sensible night's sleep is scoffed at?

There is a word in Japanese for death by overwork – *karoshi*. It is widely recognized that working for too long each day can lead to illness, stress and even death. The *American Journal of Occupational Medicine* showed that long hours can lead to hypertension, heart disease, depression, chronic infections, brain aneurisms and strokes. Alongside the detrimental effect on physical health, emotional health and relationships are adversely affected too. In one survey by the group *Parents at Work*, 64 per cent of working parents admitted that they worked longer hours than they were contracted for. Suzanne Franks comments: 'They made the familiar observation that even when there is no concrete work to be done, the way to show commitment is to stay late. Nobody dares to be the first to

---

3. Cited in Madeleine Bunting, *Willing Slaves: How the overwork culture is ruling our lives* (HarperPerennial, 2005).
4. The Chartered Management Institute, www.managers.org.uk.
5. Tim Dowling, 'Sleep tight', *Guardian*, 15 June 2006.

leave. And on top of this, when work is finished there is the all-important requirement of extra-curricular socialising, entertaining clients, attending dinners, or just going to the pub.'[6]

There are good motives for hard work, and Christians should strive for excellence in all they do, but when the fear of being the next one to be sacked, or the drive to make just that bit more money, or worry about what colleagues will think if you don't, are primary motivating factors in the amount of time spent at work, we need to be considering making a different stand.

A particular crisis for women

Alongside the general stresses that affect everyone at work, there are other more specific ones for working women, especially working mothers. The world of work has changed dramatically over the past 20 years, during which the proportion of adult women who are economically active has risen, while that for men has declined. More mothers now work: 43 per cent of women with children under five now, compared with a quarter in 1973; 46 per cent of women who work now work part-time, compared with 25 per cent in 1993.[7] However, those who are working full-time are now working harder than ever. Since 1992 there has been a leap of 52 per cent in the number of women expected to work at least 48 hours a week.[8]

Many women choose to work. The impression sometimes given that women only work when they have to is a myth. Many women work because they want to, because they enjoy it, because they've spent years training for it and because they are fulfilling their vocation. One survey revealed that seven out of ten mothers working full-time say they would work even if they didn't have to.[9] However, the pressure on women to work harder and for longer is often even greater than it is for men. The problems in

6. Franks, *Having None of It*, p. 72.
7. Institute for Employment Studies, www.employment-studies.co.uk.
8. Bunting, *Willing Slaves*.
9. Department of Trade and Industry Women and Equality Unit, www.womenand equalityunit.gov.uk.

today's working climate affect both women and men but have a particular impact on women because of their history as primary childcare providers and non-workers in the public sphere.

The challenges of balancing work and childcare

There have been heated debates about whether it is possible for women to work outside the home as well as having a fulfilling family life:

> Many of our mothers instilled in us a powerful ambition to 'make up' for the brilliant careers they missed. But they were also housewives who were 100 per cent there for us when we were children, who created loving environments from which we know we benefited. We want to provide the same stability for our children. But we are frightened of being washed up when they leave the nest. And we were educated to be fulfilled in work. So we end up stressed and frustrated.[10]

As many will testify, it is not easy being a working mother. A third of mothers taking paid maternity leave from their jobs do not return after having a baby, even if they'd like to, because they cannot work the hours they want. Professional childcare is very expensive and a woman needs to be in a highly paid job to afford it, let alone have anything left to take home for herself. For many working mothers the solution is part-time work, but there are very few part-time jobs available. On top of that, if a woman goes part-time for even a year, she will lose 10 per cent of her possible final salary.

Pulling strongly in the other direction is the emotional wrench of leaving children with other people to be looked after, and the guilt felt by many that they 'should be there for them more'. The Israeli Prime Minister Golda Meir once summed it up: 'At work, you think of the children you have left at home. At home, you

10. Camilla Cavendish, 'Was it mystique or mistake?' *The Times*, 9 February 2006.

think of the work you've left unfinished. Such a struggle is unleashed within yourself. Your heart is rent.'

The feelings of guilt are not helped by loud assertions from 'child development gurus' who state that children left in even well-run childcare will suffer all manner of emotional upset and trauma in later life. As a woman who has chosen (yes, chosen) to work, albeit mostly part-time and to have children, I can remember with great and painful clarity every new article/survey/report/edict issued about the detrimental effects of childcare. I can also report that both of my well-adjusted and happy children have been in professionally run, caring nurseries at some point in their lives and so far neither of them appears to be showing any ill effects for it. But it's a real issue for women who work, and increasingly for some men too.

The messages that come at us from the (mostly) Evangelical Christian tradition about women, men, work and children have been less than helpful. Pronouncements that women should stay at home while the head of the household goes out to work have often seemed to me to be more about maintaining a cosy cultural status quo than asserting 'biblical' principles. Studies show that the happiest marriages and the most successful families are those in which both partners are fulfilled both inside and outside the home.[11]

The pressures of 'the second shift'

The simple things of life can take so much time – filling in tax forms, cleaning the loo, filling the car up with petrol, taking the bins out, doing the shopping. For women who work outside the home, the situation is amplified. Franks regrets the fact that while many assumptions about women's roles outside the home have changed and expanded, the expectations of the work she will fulfil *at home* have stubbornly remained the same. The domestic, home-maintenance work that has been given the name 'the second shift' (by

11. See, e.g., Janice M. Steil and B. A. Turetsky, 'Is equal better?: The relationship between marital equality and psychological symptomatology', *Applied Psychology Journal* 7, ed. Stuart Oskamp (Newbury Park, California: Sage, 1987), pp. 73–97.

American sociologist Arlie Hochschild in 1989) is still mostly done by women: 'No matter what household chore is studied – washing, cooking, shopping, cleaning, childcare, the vast majority of women do more than their partner, and that includes women in full-time employment outside the home.'[12] No wonder women perceive themselves to be so busy when work doesn't stop at the end of office hours but continues in a different form when they get home.

Some women enjoy the creative and sometimes rewarding nature of making their homes nice. Some men do too. The old feminist cliché that housework is slavery and bondage and is to be shunned by all self-respecting women is less common than it used to be. We'll be exploring the particular ministry of creating and caring for a home in Chapter 7, and it's something that has the potential to appeal to both men and women.

The picture isn't as simple as saying that housework and home maintenance is boring and should therefore be shared out equally between men and women. For a start, some people don't have a partner to share it with. Women who are single, men who are single, women and men who have never had or no longer have a partner living with them do not have the option to share domestic work with someone else. However, for those women and men who do seek to live together in partnership and who both work, there are discussions to be had about who does what.

The sharing of tasks and responsibilities between women and men can lead to a greater sense of satisfaction and partnership and a decrease in stress for everyone. It's also worth bearing in mind that some people have gifts in some things and not in others. So there's no need to get ridiculous about sharing. During the seven years Mat and I job-shared and shared childcare equally, it became obvious that if either of us was to survive and if we were to eat and have clothes to wear, we would have to share in the housework and domestic tasks too. We both did the ironing, the shopping, the washing and the cleaning (apart from the few blissful years when the church paid for a cleaner for us). However, I love cooking. Mat doesn't. Mat's good with money. I'm not. So I did most of the

12. Franks, *Having None of It*, p. 108.

cooking. And he mainly dealt with the money. Stereotypical, you might say. Maybe. Oppressive? No. Sensible? I think so.

Debates rage back and forth about whether it is possible or advisable to try to combine work with any other aspect of normal, healthy life. The result is that people get more stressed and more guilty about what they aren't doing. It all paints a somewhat bleak picture. Flexible working patterns and directives on work/life balance might help. Deeper than that, though, is the way we view work at all. Christians need to develop a positive theology of work which recognizes that work is more about vocation than career. *Whatever you do*, inside or outside the home, full- or part-time, paid or voluntary, choices need to be made with wider, eternal perspectives in mind, rather than simply economic ones.

A godly perspective

So what is a Christian response to this? How could Christians make choices that might enable us to live differently in the world of work?

Work: part of God's plan

The first need is to regain a sense of God's perspective on work. Work is good and is work is godly:

> So God created humankind in his image, in the image of God he created them; male and female he created them. God blessed them, and God said to them, 'Be fruitful and multiply, and fill the earth and subdue it; and have dominion over the fish of the sea and over the birds of the air and over every living thing that moves upon the earth. (Gen. 1.27)

The first two commandments God gave to human beings were to have sex and work. We have been obsessed with both ever since!

God always intended us to work. Attitudes to work being bad spring from days of slavery (in which free people left the menial labour to slaves), and a dubious Greek dualism which stated that things of the body, like work, were to be looked down on, while higher callings of the mind, like philosophy and the arts, were championed. The Bible paints a different picture. As Mark Greene says, 'The affirmation of work pervades scripture.'[13] So, for example, we read in Eccl. 2.24–26: 'There is nothing better for mortals than to eat and drink, and find enjoyment in their toil. This also, I saw, is from the hand of God; for apart from him who can eat or who can have enjoyment?' Work is good, sanctioned and blessed by God and intended as an integral part of human existence.

There is at the moment a revival of interest in the spirituality of the first Christians in Britain, the Celtic Christians. The Celtic view of life was that there was no division between the sacred and the secular, the ordinary and the holy. All of life was to be lived in God's service and all life (people as well as nature) was permeated with the image of God. Celtic Christians had prayers for every aspect of everyday life, including work. They had prayers for sheep shearing, weaving, fishing and farming, lighting a fire, making a bed, milking a cow.[14]

In this way of thinking, work is not a burden, but a blessing to be embraced as a gift of God. Perhaps someone needs to write some Celtic prayers for today's work – typing, word processing, driving, filing, changing nappies, that will help us to see all work as God's gift, filled with his presence and worthy of his blessing.

Work: a vocation

The word 'vocation' stems from the Latin root 'vocare', meaning 'to call'. Work is a response to a summons. Every person has a calling from God to do something, whether it be outside the home or in it, voluntarily or for payment: 'God invites everyone to make

---

13. Mark Greene, *Thank God it's Monday* (Scripture Union, 1988), p. 32.
14. See, for example, Esther de Waal, *The Recovery of the Religious Imagination* (Bantam Doubleday Dell, 1997).

some contribution to the life of the world, some piece of gift-work or service to others, that only you can do because of the particular person you are, your gifts, your wounds, your personal background and history. It will be something that expresses the unique essence of what you are, which God calls out from you to be a gift to others.'[15]

It used to be felt that the only 'true' vocation was to the ordained, missionary or religious life, that your vocation was what you did at church and that the secular workplace didn't really count. Thankfully, Christians are increasingly realizing that every person has a unique vocation, and that there is no higher calling in the Church than in the secular world of work. If you are called to be a teacher, or an accountant, or a doctor, or a parent at home with children, or a vicar, that is your Christian vocation – the way you serve God's purposes in the world.

There are people who have come to speak to me about whether or not God might be calling them to full-time ordained ministry. It has become clear in the course of the conversation that he is not, not because they aren't gifted enough, or capable enough to do the job of a vicar. Quite the opposite. Some of them would have made superb vicars. They were not called, however, because they were very good teachers, or very good lawyers, or very good social workers, and God needs good teachers and lawyers and social workers to do his work in the world just as much as he needs good vicars (maybe more!).

One effect of a having a theology of calling is that it becomes more possible to see your job (or your time spent caring for relatives, or children, or volunteering, or studying) as a means of living out your relationship with God and his world.

If we believe that God has a unique plan for each person he has made, a mission, if you like, we will be living life to the full if we follow that calling. That calling might involve many different factors – and that's what makes life busy. I believe I am called to be a follower of Jesus, a wife, mother, priest, writer, amongst other things. The knack is finding out what combination of things *you* are called to be doing (as opposed to the person next door).

15. Francis Dewar, 'God calls everyone', www.cofeanglican.org/ministry.

It is very easy to look around you and see what others are doing and wonder if you should be doing the same. I think this is particularly true in the debate about whether to stay at home with children or go out to work. I detect in many instances a kind of one-upmanship in those who have made either one choice or the other, possibly arising out of a temptation to feel guilty about what you're *not* doing. There is a story in the Gospel of John that deals with this feeling in one of the Jesus's disciples.

It is shortly after Jesus's Resurrection, and he is on the beach with his friends. Jesus is explaining to Peter something of his calling: 'Feed my sheep. Very truly, I tell you, when you were younger, you used to fasten your own belt and to go wherever you wished. But when you grow old, you will stretch out your hands, and someone else will fasten a belt around you and take you where you do not wish to go.' (He said this to indicate the kind of death by which he would glorify God.) After this he said to him, 'Follow me.' Peter turned and saw the disciple whom Jesus loved following them; he was the one who had reclined next to Jesus at the supper and had said, 'Lord, who is it that is going to betray you?'. When Peter saw him, he said to Jesus, 'Lord, what about him?' Jesus said to him, 'If it is my will that he remain until I come, what is that to you? Follow me!' (Jn 21.17–19).

Peter was not content with knowing what his own calling was. He wanted to know where John fitted into the picture too. Maybe he wanted to weigh up his own calling against what John would be asked to do, in order to give validation to his own relationship with Jesus. It's easy to do that – to look at what someone else is doing and wonder if it is better, or more godly, or more right, than what you are doing. 'That's not the way,' Jesus says. 'What is it to you if I have asked that person to go out to work, or that person to stay at home with children? You must follow me in *your* own calling.'

The tricky thing is that vocations might change over time. Mat used to be called to be a chemical engineer. Then God called him into ordained ministry. An added complication is that many of us are called to be several different things at once, which can lead some of us to feel overwhelmed and over-busy. The key thing is learning to hear God's voice. When we are occupied doing whatever it is God has asked us to do, we have the potential to be fulfilled and at peace with our lot. Eric Hoffer said: 'The feeling of being hurried is not usually the result of living a full life and having no time. It is on the contrary born of a vague fear that we are wasting our life. When we do not do the one thing we ought to do, we have no time for anything else – we are the busiest people in the world.'[16] The converse is also true. When we do do the one thing we ought to do, we have time for everything. Sounds great doesn't it? But that's easier said than done. Even St Paul expressed his exasperation with not doing what he thought he should be doing: 'I can will what is right, but I cannot do it. For I do not do the good I want, but the evil I do not want is what I do' (Rom. 7.18–19).

So what should you do?

Discerning vocation is not easy, especially as God seems to delight in calling us to things that we never thought would be in our capabilities to do. I remember very well that feeling when God first called me to ordained ministry. I was six months pregnant with our daughter. I had begun to have a sneaking suspicion that God might be asking me to be a priest, mainly through what other people had said to me, but the fact that I was young, female and pregnant made the idea seem faintly ridiculous. At that time I didn't know many women who were ordained, let alone young, pregnant ones.

Then one Advent I went to a service at our church in which the reading was all about Mary's visit from Gabriel, who asked her to be the mother of God's son. 'Let it be to me as you have said,' she said, despite the ridiculous, precarious, dangerous and radical nature of the thing she was being asked to do. I came away from that service feeling that God hadn't asked me to bear his son (thank goodness). He was only asking me to be a vicar, so what was I making a fuss about? And I realized that night that God did use young, pregnant women in his plans.

At several points along the way I have been apprehensive about what my calling to this kind of ministry was going to mean for myself and – more often – my children. Soon after I arrived at

16. Eric Hoffer, *Reflections on the Human Condition* (HarperCollins, 1973), aphorism 156.

theological college I expressed this fear to one of the tutors, a wise man who said to me that if God was calling me to this walk of life, which I believed he was, then he was calling my children too. God had a joined-up view of life, and what was right for me was right for my family. He read me a verse from Isa. 40.11: 'He will feed his flock like a shepherd; he will gather the lambs in his arms, and carry them in his bosom, and gently lead the mother sheep.' That gentle picture of a God who leads, not drives, and who protects those who have little ones to care for, has continued to be a great source of reassurance for me.

The point is this: if God calls you to do something for him, he will equip you for it. As it says in 1 Thess. 5.24: 'The one who calls you is faithful, and he will do this.' If our vocation comes from God, he will take care of the potential complications, including those to do with family and children. I have spoken to many women who have sensed God calling them into some kind of church leadership, but who have been anxious about what it might mean for their families. What I always say to them is that he who calls them will be faithful to them and to their families if they step out and take the risky steps in his strength. Stephen Ferns, the vocations officer for the Church of England, says this: 'God never calls us to be something or someone we're not. God always calls us to what we are capable of becoming ... It may be that we have hidden gifts which need to be discovered or it may be that there is something that we have secretly always wanted to do but have not had the courage or the time to try.'[17]

So how do you discern your vocation? Or more accurately, how do you *hear* vocation? For if vocation is calling it follows that someone is doing the calling and our task is to hear and respond.

Firstly, spend time discovering what your passion is, what makes you tick, what you're good at, what you were trained for, what you might do further study in, what you are skilled at doing – and what you would like to do. My experience is that people often discount that last one. What would you *like* to do, given the choice? There is a slightly warped Christian ethos that says, 'If I like doing something, it can't be what God wants me to do. In

17. Stephen Ferns, 'Called to be you', www.cofe.anglican.org ministry.

order to be doing God's will, it must be really painful and nasty.' Where does that idea come from? Yes, God does sometimes call us to lay down our preferences and to make sacrifices for him, but not always in the ways we are expecting. We often forget that God is on our side and does want us to enjoy life, if at all possible!

When I was exploring the call to ordained ministry in the Church, I remember finding it odd that I actually *wanted* to do it. I had spoken with so many people whose calling to ordination had been a struggle, a wrestling of their wills against God's. They didn't really want to do it (or so they said) but God had insisted. So I thought that actually quite fancying the idea of being a vicar must be evidence that I wasn't hearing God correctly. Then I went on a conference for people discerning a call to ordained ministry and one of the first things the woman running the course said was that God often works through our hearts and wills. What we enjoy (or think we might enjoy) may be exactly what he is calling us to. I nearly wept with relief! God is able to call to us through our wills in line with his, our heartbeat in time with his. So if you really like doing something, pay careful consideration to it as a possible calling of God.

There are many courses and schemes now available to help you discover your vocation. But one of the most trusted ways of discerning vocation is simply by talking it through with others, by listening to God and by being open to hear his voice speaking through them. There is really no substitute for mulling it over in a prayerful way with those whose opinion you trust. Discovering meaning and purpose for your life is not likely to come through bolts of lightning from on high (although it might), or in an instant (although it might). It is more likely to be a long process of listening to God's voice, in your heart, your soul, your mind, your passions and in other people. It is likely to involve hard work, some trial and error, always choice, and sometimes courage.

Find that thing that you are meant to be doing, and trust God for the rest – money, children, housing, pension, and so on. Make the decisions based on what you believe you should be doing with your life and don't listen to the voices that instil guilt and doubt.

Work: an act of co-creation with God

God made us in his image to be creative and one of the ways we reflect this is in the creativity we bring to our work. This sense of creativity might be easier to see if you are a painter or poet, a nanny or a care-worker, but perhaps more difficult if you work behind the tills in Tesco. The fact is, though, that our work is one of the ways in which we participate in the creative power of God in ordering, shaping and forming the world.

Whether or not the creative power of God is immediately visible in every aspect of your daily grind, it is possible to allow everything you do to bring glory to God and to see God in your work at every point. If all of life belongs to God, it follows that God's grace can be found in everything, even daily chores. Mundane tasks such as hoovering or marking essays can be done as a service to God and as a means of his blessing. George Herbert expresses this in his poem 'The Elixir' which begins: 'Teach me, my God and King,/In all things thee to see,/And what I do in any thing,/To do it as for thee.' In that poem he speaks of committing even the most mundane of tasks to God: 'Who sweeps a room, as for thy laws,/Makes that and th' action fine.'

A healthy view of work might include the perspective that you are playing a part with God in the care and sustenance of the world he has made and is making. God has no hands and feet and lips in this world other than in the people he has made. If he wants to do anything about practically taking care of the world he must do it through us. So if your work is to look after small children at home, you are doing the work of God in raising a healthy and happy person. If your work is farming, you are doing the work of God by taking care of the earth and producing crops to feed people. It is not just Christians who can do the work of God. Goodness is not the preserve of those who follow Christ. I believe that God has put that spark of co-creation into every heart and mind. Not everyone chooses to use it wisely, but there are many who do.

Work as worship

I learned a lot about work at Lee Abbey. People join the community to work. They are also called by God to grow in their faith, to live in community and to serve the guests, but one of the ways in which they do that is through the work that they do. Most of the work at Lee Abbey is fairly menial, and not necessarily what people have been trained for. Some of the longer-term members, like chaplain, catering manager, estate manager, are doing what they've been trained to do, but for the vast majority of community members, their work is more basic than their qualifications and abilities. They would not, in another context, choose to do these unskilled tasks in the workplace. The work they do is not really a brilliant 'career move', and yet they see it as their vocation for that time.

New community members are asked to make promises to the rest of the community about their intended commitment to the common life. One of them is this: 'Do you intend to make the weekly corporate Communion the central act of your *work* and worship? The work of the community is very much part of its worship and offering to God, in the way expressed by Rom. 12.1, "Therefore, I urge you, brothers and sisters, in view of God's mercy, to offer your bodies as living sacrifices, holy and pleasing to God – this is your spiritual act of worship".' Promising to make the weekly Communion the central act of work *and* worship encompasses all that is expressed by communal living; faith, corporate commitment – and work. There is no separation between the sacred and the secular, the holy and the practical. Work is worship and worship is work. As one community member expressed it: 'Worshipping with those I spend my week working with makes the experience more meaningful.'

How easy is it to see our work – what we do – as part of our worship of God? If we are to realize Jesus's offer of life in all its fullness, the way we see our daily work, and what it does to our emotional and spiritual lives, is of key importance. The trouble is that many Christians have not been encouraged to see work as part of their Christian life, or as something that interests God. Of course God wants me in church on a Sunday, but he isn't interested in what I do on a Monday morning is he? Actually yes, he is very interested.

At a licensing service for a new vicar, the bishop ended the service by saying:

> We have all made a fuss of the new vicar because he's starting a new job. We have commissioned and licensed him for his work. Wouldn't it be wonderful if all of you who work in other areas outside the Church were commissioned and licensed in the same way when you started new jobs? Because that is your ministry.

He's absolutely right. All of our work, whether paid or unpaid, full or part-time, church-based or secular, is our mission and our ministry. It is ordinary Christians living out their calling where God places them day by day.

But we do not live out that calling alone. God places us alongside other people to work. One of the ways in which God works most creatively is in the partnership between men and women in all areas. It is a partnership that does not always come easily and to which we now turn.

Partnership and sacrifice

Men and women at work

If, as we have seen in Genesis ch. 1, God originally intended men and women to work together to 'fill the earth and subdue it', it follows that men and women should today be living out the same kind of shared vocation. Why is it, then, that so much time and energy is today given to the task of helping men and women to work together well? Whole government departments are devoted to it. Books have been written about it. Companies hold management training exercises to help male and female employees work together better. What's the problem? The trouble is that many thousands of years of discrimination, exploitation, manipulation, oppression and harassment between women and men in the workplace have passed since Genesis 1. There is a lot that still needs to be worked on concerning gender relations at work.

Where men and women work together well today, the restoring, redeeming work of God is advanced a little more. I have had the privilege of working closely with several men in the course of my ministry as a priest. Prophesies of gloom and doom told to me before my ordination about the prejudice I would experience in the Church of England have not been fulfilled. I know that this is not true for all women priests, but I have had some wonderful male colleagues. What is the secret of men and women working well together in partnership? I have neither the space nor the remit to go into this tricky issue in much detail here. I simply offer a couple of pointers from my own experience.

I think the number one thing is not to be threatened by difference, but to embrace it as part of God's rich provision – and that includes difference in gender. Most men I have worked with have enjoyed the richness that having men and women in the same team brings, a quality that may be lacking in single-sex teams. Secondly, men and women at work need to learn to play to each other's individual strengths and gifts, and these need not be limited by gender. As we allocated tasks in the chaplaincy team at Lee Abbey, it was done according to gifts and skills, not gender. So a man might be given a more pastoral job if that was his strength, while women were often to be found teaching large groups and house parties, if they were the more competent communicators. Thirdly, and most importantly, men and women at work need to learn to be friends, as well as colleagues – to enjoy each other's company in an attitude of respecting and valuing each other. I would always rather work in a mixed male and female team because of the richness and variety it brings and because men and women working together more fully reflect the image of God.

Occupation

Working parents

It is possible for men and women to relate to each other well at work. But what about where the two people who work happen to be married to each other? As we saw earlier in that rather depressing picture of the state of working life in Britain today, one of the biggest challenges is for families where both parents work.

One of my favourite books is by Allison Pearson. *I Don't Know How She Does It* is about a woman, Kate Reddy, who tries to juggle a high-powered career with a home and family life. I loved the hilarious descriptions of her attempts to be perfect at everything (like bashing mince pies bought from Marks and Spencer with a spoon, in order to fool other mothers into thinking they are home-made). As Kate struggles with combining work and motherhood, the solution for her in the end is not to go part-time, or to move to a smaller house and get a job with more realistic hours, or even for her husband to do more at home, but for her to give up work altogether. She gives these reasons for her decision:

Reasons to give up work:

1. Because I have got two lives and I don't have time to enjoy either of them
2. Because 24 hours are not enough
3. Because my children will only be young for a short time
4. Because one day I caught my husband looking at me the way my mother used to look at my father
5. Because becoming a man is a waste of a woman
6. Because I am too tired to think of another because[18]

As I read that, I feel slightly disappointed that in the end she couldn't work it out, with her husband, and that it had to come to that. But I understand – completely. It *is* difficult for families where both parents work, but the answer all too often seems to be for women to give up work in order to concentrate on what goes on at home. Don't get me wrong: for some women, it is right to give up

18. Allison Pearson, *I Don't Know How She Does It* (Vintage, 2003), p. 341.

work if and when they have children. But I can't help wondering if some women give up their worked-hard-for careers when they would rather not have done, simply because the pressure of juggling becomes too much when the men in their lives are not prepared to take up their share of the domestic responsibility. There are many partnerships where the decision to 'stay at home' is made not out of any sense of reasoned choice and calling, but out of a stereotypical assumption that it is the women's work that has to go.

A recent article in the *Guardian* carried interviews with several fathers who had chosen to shorten their working hours in order to share childcare responsibilities with their working wives. One of them said: 'Looking after the children a couple of days a week means that I get to know them really well. I have good, supportive colleagues at work and I find work less stressful because I'm now at home for more days of the week than I'm at work.'[19]

Suzanne Franks says this about working women: 'The only ones who have pulled through are the ones whose husbands have done more than their share but they are rare, because this is rubbing up against all the same stereotypes. Things are changing so much more slowly than our generation anticipated.'[20] Likewise Tessa Jowell, the Secretary of State for Culture, Media and Sport, spoke recently about the pressures on women when they have children and work. She suggested that the responsibility for family and for work was ideally a shared one between father and mother, man and woman, husband and wife – which is where men come in:

> In the longer term there are a number of things that will begin to close the pay gap and perhaps the most interesting is the greater sharing by men of parental responsibility ... As men do more at home, women can do more at work. That, I think, is the next stage of the revolution. It's a stage that may be laughed at by older men, but most young men will [do it] – they want to be more part of their children's lives than their own fathers were part of theirs.[21]

19. Diane Taylor, 'Daddy's home', *Guardian*, 24 April 2006.
20. Franks, *Having None of It*, quoted in Maureen Freely, 'Can mothers make it work?', *Observer*, 28 April 2002.
21. Tessa Jowell, quoted in *Observer*, 27 November 2005.

Far from being an impossible ideal, likely to cause more stress, research has shown that sharing tasks at home, childcare and work might actually lead to greater levels of happiness for both husband and wife. Research carried out in Sweden has shown that shared work and childcare leads to higher levels of perceived well-being, over and above families where only one parent works and families where two parents work but one carries most of the domestic responsibility. The study concludes that 'multiple roles and shared responsibilities and demands in the private sphere promote health among both women and men'.[22] That's a rather long-winded way of saying that a good way of functioning as a family is partnership between the husband and wife, in work, in the family and in domestic responsibility – just as intended in Genesis 1.

There is a lot of work to be done in challenging the stereotypes. Our decision to job-share and to share the care of our children really began in earnest when our son arrived and I returned to take up the half share of the curacy work I had left just before he was born. That meant that Mat was often to be found taking Toby to toddler group, shopping for the evening meal and picking our older daughter up from school, while I worked. At other times the roles were reversed. Mat lost count of the number of times he was stopped by a well-meaning parishioner, as he pushed the pram around our neighbourhood: 'Where's Emma. Is she *all right?*', as if the alarming situation of Toby's father caring for his own son during daylight hours must have been necessitated only by some dire affliction having befallen the child's mother.

I am not saying that this partnership thing is the answer to all our problems of overwork and busyness. There are larger factors at work to do with economics, market forces, deeply ingrained patterns of employment and attitudes that cannot be solved in glib pro-nouncements about changing stereotypes. But you have to make a start somewhere. And it's not working now. So you can decide what you are going to do about it *today*. We won't be able to change it all overnight, but now is the place to start. That way, we might not be able to 'have it all', but to have the life that God intended for each of us. Sharing work, home life and parenting is not always an

22. E. Bejerot Harenstam, *International Journal of Social Welfare* (Blackwell Synergy, 2001).

easy choice. Discerning what it is you are meant to be doing will almost certainly involve the converse process of discerning what it is you're *not* meant to be doing too. This might involve sacrifice, as it did for Jesus. It is not possible for everyone to do everything, so choices have to be made, laying down our lives for the other.

Those dads I mentioned earlier who were sharing childcare with their partners all mentioned what they had given up, as well as what they had gained: 'We have taken a financial hit and are both earning 60 per cent of what we were earning three years ago'; 'I earn about three-quarters of what I would be earning if I was a full-time GP, but for me it's worth taking the pay cut because my quality of life is so much better'; 'I have to accept that working less will have an impact on my progress, but I don't really mind that'. What they have expressed is the fact that there is more to life than money and what they have gained outweighs what they have lost.

Stepping above

There is a crisis in the world of work. I believe one of the answers is for men and women, for husbands and wives in particular, but for all for men and women in the workplace to support each other better, to communicate with each other better and to see any partnership or family as a unit, not as a competition. We need to show something different – making choices about the way we occupy our time that give equal importance to the vocations of men and women.

So how might all this make a difference to your busy life? What might living differently in the world of work mean for you?

A different partnership between men and women

For some women it might mean including yourself as part of the solution more, and realizing that your vocation is just as important as that of the man standing next to you. For some men it might involve a laying down of some things you have thought of as your 'right'. For some men it might mean challenging assumptions about what it means to be a man, especially in the workplace. A report on fathers in the workplace[23] concludes that while many women have learned to ask for flexible work practices in order to accommodate family life, many men have not yet developed the confidence to do so, preferring to take time off 'by stealth', rather than admitting their needs as fathers. Many men 'lack the tools and language' to ask for flexible work.[24]

A different partnership may mean men learning to be proud of the lives they lead outside as well as inside the workplace and learning to express their needs in both areas. It may mean increased negotiation between men and women in the home, husbands and wives and partners talking honestly together about vocation, and how both might be fulfilled. It may mean better representing the views and skills of men and women at all levels in the workplace. It may mean encouraging women into more senior positions of leadership. It may mean simply breaking down stereotypes that restrict men or women to one profession or another. I have a friend who is finding it very hard to get a post as a nursery teacher. This person is well qualified, competent and able. And he is a man. He fears the reason for his not getting jobs often is his maleness.

A different perspective on work

Living differently in the world of work might simply mean refusing to let your work take over your whole life to such an extent that it is the cause of stress to yourself and your family, instead of being a source of fulfilment and provision in your life. It might mean choosing to take all your holidays, or a decent lunch hour, in order to rest and recuperate. It might mean going home before everyone else in the office does. It might mean standing up

---

23. 'Dad's Army: The case for father-friendly workplaces', by Richard Reeves of the Work Foundation, www.theworkfoundation.com.
24. Cited in Andy Lake, 'Superdads', in the online business journal *Flexibility*, www.flexibility.co.uk.

against 'the system'. It might mean accepting lower standards of living as a consequence.

Find practical ways of slowing down at work. I have heard the suggestion that you can use some of the natural waiting moments that come in the course of a day as a point at which to stop, perhaps pray, or simply reflect – the time a computer takes to load a program, the time a phone takes to ring before you answer it, the time the kettle takes to boil. All of these can be small moments of peace in the midst of the busyness, if we look at them in that light.

It may be also that you want to take some time out to ask some serious questions of your work, your vocation and the way you spend your time. Start with a relatively small space of time in which to do this – perhaps half an hour every week, where you ask yourself questions such as: What is it that's most complicating my life? Am I working too hard? Am I working at a job I don't like? What is draining my energy? Then start thinking about how and what you can cut back. Book a retreat. Make an appointment to talk to a wise friend, take a long walk with the specific purpose of reflecting on your working life.

For some people, living well with work might mean saying 'ya boo sucks' to a system that demands you work longer and longer hours at the expense of your sanity and your relationships. It might mean saying, 'Yes, I enjoy my work and I like being fully occupied, but I am not prepared to sacrifice my life and soul to it.'

Now, where should I start . . .?

Spirituality and busyness

4

How do we find time for our spiritual lives as well as everything else?

I suspect prayer is one of the areas about which Christians feel most guilt (alongside thinking wrong thoughts about sex, eating too much chocolate and not spending enough time playing interesting, educational games with our children). I wonder if I am the only one who knows I need to pray, wants to pray more even, but struggles to find the time and (if I'm really honest) the motivation to do so. The other day I told my husband I was writing the chapter for my book on prayer. I said, 'But I'm the worst person to do that. I'm rubbish at prayer.' He said (he's very sensible at times), 'No, that means you're the best person to do it. Many people who are reading your book will feel they're rubbish at prayer too.'

Do you? If so, join me in the admission that we don't do very well at it, and in the commitment to find a realistic, fruitful, worthwhile, sustainable way of doing it better that *really* works in our busy lives.

Messages

There is a great longing for stillness and silence these days. We are seeing an increased awareness of and interest in spirituality. There is a thirst amongst many for a quieter life, for a chance to get in touch with the deeper places within. They want quiet, or feel that they need quiet. They're looking for an escape from busy lives. Very popular this past year have been two television series, *The Monastery* and *The Convent*, about groups of men and women going to live in a monastery and a convent respectively. The people featured in these programmes were busy, active, 'worldly' people who wanted to capture something they felt they had either lost or never had. Most of them gained a huge amount from their time spent in the quiet, contemplative spirituality of monastic life.

The burgeoning 'spirituality' industry with its increased emphasis on the inner life as well as the outer is a much needed rediscovery of the fact that we are more than just bodies and minds, that we have souls too. Yet I can't help wondering if it is yet another source of pressure on busy people. It used to be OK just to be busy. Now you have to be spiritual, and find time to explore the inner reaches of your soul, as well. There's another thing to add to the To Do List: Get soul sorted out. Go on retreat. Spend time in prayer.

Some books about how to improve your prayer life suggest that you have to get less busy before your prayer life will fall into place. There may be a lot of truth in the fact that we are too busy for many things, including prayer, but to suggest that if we all just slow down prayer would come naturally is, for many of us, to dream an impossible dream as well as to misunderstand what prayer is. Sometimes there is the implication that quiet and withdrawal are the *only* prerequisites for spiritual health. Many people have bought the notion that it is *only* in silence and solitude that we find God. Consequently, there are people who sincerely believe that they have to disconnect from their real lives to connect with God.

But this is not so. When your schedule is crazy, it's tempting to say to yourself, 'When it calms down, when this is all over, I'll ...' But this – the busyness, the chaos – is life, too. It's part of the script. It's more than something you have to get through while you're waiting for cherished quiet time or that retreat you booked months ago.

> Prayer fits awkwardly into a busy life. The very word 'prayer' resonates with slowing down, sitting still, shutting our eyes. It doesn't fit with quick responses and one-line emails, with crowded trains, demanding children, fussing colleagues, deadlines and targets. Prayer ends up swept into hasty getting-up and sleepy last-before-lights-out times.[1]

1. Margaret Killingray, 'The priority of prayer', *Word for the Week* 16 October 2006, www.licc.org.uk.

If we believe that our primary relationship is with the God who made us and redeems us, devoting time to this relationship should be the most natural thing in the world. We are creatures made by God and made to need sustenance for our souls as well as our bodies. William Wilberforce, the Christian statesman of the late eighteenth and early nineteenth centuries, once said: 'I must secure more time for private devotions. I have been living far too public for me. The shortening of private devotions starves the soul. It grows lean and faint.' We are whole people, body, mind and spirit, and we need to feed all three, even when – especially when – we are very busy.

There is a paradox about praying. Like any skill or art it needs to be practised, nurtured and honed. It is something you can get better at with time and attention and worse at with neglect. But prayer is also very simply the way in which we commune with our Maker and should therefore be as natural as breathing. You don't think about breathing that much, you just do it automatically because you need to stay alive. When you are in a hurry and a rush, you breathe more rapidly. The more you exert yourself, the more life-giving oxygen your body needs and your breaths come faster. If prayer is like breathing, it should follow that as we are busier, we pray more and with more urgency, because we need to, to stay alive spiritually.

Many Christian writers today are expressing the truth that in this fast-paced, quick-fix, superficial culture in which we live, Christians need to model something different, deeper and more thoughtful. Richard Foster expresses it like this: 'Superficiality is the curse of our age. The doctrine of instant satisfaction is a primary spiritual problem. The desperate need today is not for a great number of intelligent people, or gifted people, but for deep people.'[2] I couldn't agree more. The trouble is I think we often assume that 'deep' and 'busy' must necessarily be opposites; that it is not possible to be a deeply spiritual person and to be a busy person at the same time.

I have spent most of my Christian life struggling and failing to be a 'spiritual' person. Much of what I have read and heard about how

2. Richard Foster, *Celebration of Discipline* (Hodder and Stoughton, 1998).

to be godly has been written about and spoken by people who are deeply contemplative, quiet introverts who enjoy spending 'time alone in their cell', as it were. I admire them deeply, but I am not really that kind of person.

The image that comes to my mind when I think of the phrase (so often used in Christian circles) 'spending time with God' is of a person kneeling alone in a room for hours on end, in silence, thinking holy thoughts. I'd rather stick pins in myself. I am an activist, a busy person. I tell myself I should have a quiet time, but I have neither time nor quietness. I try to fit it in. I fail. I feel guilty and the cycle starts again. It has come as a revelation to me in recent years to find that, on one level, that's OK. It's OK to struggle with silence and stillness. God has made us all different. Some people engage with him in quietness and contemplation. Others find him in the rush and the excitement.

In John Ortberg's excellent book about finding God in everyday life, *God is Closer than You Think*, he points out that people have different 'spiritual pathways' – ways in which they most naturally engage with God: 'the way we most naturally sense God's presence and experience spiritual growth'.[3] Some find God through intellectual pursuit and reason, others through worship in abandon, others in stillness and contemplation, others through the beauty of creation and still others through activity and passionate energy. He cites great biblical characters like Nehemiah, who found themselves closest to God in the middle of the busyness (what could be busier than rebuilding Jerusalem?). I found it fascinating to note the sense of release I felt in being told it was OK for me to relate to God in one way (through activity and through study, mainly) and for another person to relate to God in an entirely different way. I found it releasing and inspiring to know that it was acceptable to be a naturally active person, that it's the way God made me, and that there are ways of connecting with God in the fast lane. I know I need to slow down sometimes, we all do, but it is very comforting to know that when I'm racing along, God doesn't fall off.

The more I talked to fellow members of the Lee Abbey community about this, the more I found it was a great release for a lot

3. John Ortberg, *God is Closer than You Think* (Zondervan, 2005), p. 121.

of people. Lee Abbey is a place where people often come for quietness and retreat. We had week-long silent retreats several times a year (usually populated by clapped-out clergy) and other weekends that focused on silence and quiet devotional prayer. Yet many of the community I spoke to found they did not relate to God easily like this. Many admitted struggling with silence. Once I had told them (as a good chaplain should) that silence was something valuable and that we all have to learn to be more comfortable with it (I do think this – honestly), I got to talking with them about different ways *they* found for relating to God and speaking to him. For many of them, I heard, it was the beautiful 300-acre estate around the house at Lee Abbey that was the greatest source of spiritual inspiration. Some of them found God in the arts – dancing, drama, music. Some of them said that that, like me, they felt most spiritually alive when they were actively engaged in tasks and jobs – as long as these were tasks they experienced as part of their godly vocation.

It made me think that we don't often see advertised at Lee Abbey, or anywhere else, retreats for activists, retreats for people who like being busy, retreats for people who find God most naturally in the faces and words of other people rather than alone, retreats for people who like to be on the go. Perhaps we should call them 'Advances' rather than 'Retreats'!

The world of 'the very spiritual' seems littered with people who naturally really like silence, introverts who enjoy spending time on their own, who'd rather not be too busy, who find contemplation easy. Where are the people who like to be active, who enjoy having a full diary, who thrive on lots of interaction, and yet find God in the midst of their busyness? As Ortberg says, '... all too often we fail to realise that our individual uniqueness means we will all experience God's presence and learn to relate to him in different ways, in ways that correspond to the wiring patterns he himself has created in us.'[4]

4. Ibid.

A godly perspective

Not everyone in the Bible prayed about the same things or in the same way. There do not seem to be many blueprints about the 'right way to do it' (with the possible exception of Jesus's teaching on the Lord's Prayer in Luke ch. 10). The Bible is full of stories about people who prayed 'on the go' and while they were active, often doing what God has asked them to do in the first place! Adam and Eve prayed as they walked with God in the cool of the evening in the Garden of Eden (praying must have been much easier with God physically walking beside you). David prays for himself as he confronts his enemies (Psalm 25), Daniel prays from the lion's den, Jonah from the belly of the whale, and so on.

Jesus and prayer

Wherever Jesus went, people crowded around him, constantly asking for things, and he responded – healing, teaching, touching, giving. Jesus prayed on the run in every situation in which he found himself. Jesus prayed because he needed to and prayer really did seem to be for him as natural as breathing. He prayed for discernment, he prayed for his disciples (Lk. 22.32; John 17; Jn 14.16), he prayed in anguish for strength to complete the mission he had been given (Lk. 22.44). He prayed in many different places – at the graveside of his friend who had died (Jn 11.41), on the hillside before people eating (Mk. 8.6–7; Jn 6.11 and 23; Mk. 14.22), in small groups (Lk. 11.1; Lk. 9.18). He prayed sitting (Mt. 26.26), lying face downwards (Mt. 26.39) and looking to heaven (Jn 17.1). Jesus seems to pray in ways that are provoked by what is going on around him at the time. He prays out of his experience as it progresses.

As well as praying on the go, Jesus was also good at withdrawing to be on his own to pray. He sought times of solitude and silence when he prayed alone: 'In the morning, while it was still very dark, he got up and went out to a deserted place, and there he prayed. And Simon and his companions hunted for him' (Mk 1.35). In fact, Jesus sought time in solitude and prayer before every important decision and action in his public ministry. Before he began his public ministry he spent 40 days alone with God in the wilderness. He spent a night in prayer before choosing his 12 disciples. He withdrew to the Mount of Transfiguration to prepare for the final journey to Jerusalem. Before he went to the Cross he spent time in weeping and prayer at Gethsemane. Jesus prayed a lot in many different ways and situations, but it was as if he knew that before he did anything major, he needed time alone with God, in preparation for all that was to come.

Perhaps this provides a good model of prayer for other busy people. We need to learn to pray both on the hoof, wherever we find ourselves, as well as having times of silence and solitude, even if those things don't come easily.

There is a school of thought that says we must put aside time daily to spend in prayer. Of course there is a lot of truth in this, and it would be lovely, but I know many deeply committed, spiritually mature Christians who really struggle with both the idea and the practical reality of finding time *daily* to set aside to pray. One of the hardest periods of life to do this kind of regular praying is when you have very young children. I remember when my children were tiny, listening to a preacher who told me that if I was not setting aside half an hour daily to spend in prayer, I should get up half an hour earlier. At the time my daughter was waking me up at 5 a.m. 'On your bike', I thought.

The answer may not be to have *daily* times of solitude and prayer. It may not even be to have *frequent* times of solitude and prayer but to have *regular* times of solitude and prayer. Regular might mean once a week. It might mean at times of significance, coupled with a keen sense of God's presence 'on the run'. Perhaps for busy people, the particular time for withdrawing in a longer period of time alone for prayer is, like Jesus, not every day, but before major events and decisions.

It's like any relationship. If our relationship with God is ignored totally it will perish. Mat and I most of the time just *are* with each other. We live together and we parent together and we see each other in the busyness of everyday life. Our conversation usually consists of things like 'Will you put the rubbish out?' and 'Who's picking up the kids?' Not the stuff of dreams, but necessary. That is the main thing that maintains, develops and deepens our relationship. We try to set aside an evening a week where we have a meal together alone. That helps too. Once a year we try and go away for a weekend together. That's a great boost to our relationship as well.

Perhaps it's like that with God. Most of the time we just live with him, and make sure we recognize his presence in our homes and our lives, chatting with him all the time. That is praying and that's the main way I do it, so I've decided to stop feeling guilty about it. Occasionally I set aside a longer time to pray. And then once a year or so I may go away for an extended time alone with God.

Although I don't find this kind of prolonged withdrawal at all easy, I know I have benefited from praying like this at key times in my life. Before I was ordained as a priest, all of us curates were expected to spend a time on silent retreat at the diocesan retreat centre. It was really inconvenient for me. We then had a five-year-old and a five-month-old whom I was still breastfeeding. Fortunately the retreat centre was just down the road from our house. I was given special dispensation to sleep at home, my wonderful mother looked after the baby during the day and I popped home at regular intervals to feed him. It's not the way I would recommend doing silent retreats! However, despite the less than ideal circumstances, I would say it is one of the times I met with God most clearly and discernibly. I believe I was equipped during those days of silence (and whizzing back and forward to breastfeed!) for all that my priestly ministry has been.

Prayer and busyness can go together

'Busyness and prayer' are not an oxymoron. Being busy makes all the more important the need for prayer. And vice versa. Fervent prayer is a busy activity – and will probably lead to more busyness, as our heroes of the Bible found. Esther de Waal says in her introduction to the spirituality of the Benedictines: 'Prayer is the anchor which brings the inner strength to my daily activity; my daily activity informs that prayer and anchors it in the reality of today's world.'[5] If we are busy people there is all the more need for the deepening that prayer brings. It is what is behind the exhortation in Paul's letter to the Thessalonians to 'Rejoice always, pray without ceasing, give thanks in all circumstances' (1 Thess. 5.16–18).

Prayer in the busyness

So let's look at praying on the go, in the middle of the rush.

God is not just in church, not just where Christians gather, not just in worship, although he is in those places. The presence of God is everywhere around us – in the created world, in your home, in your family, in your friends, in the supermarket, at your place of work. C.S. Lewis said this: 'We may ignore, but we can nowhere evade, the presence of God. The world is crowded with him.'[6] Gerard Manley Hopkins said: 'The world is charged with the grandeur of God . . .'[7] The Psalmist puts it like this: 'Where can I go from your Spirit? Where can I flee from your presence? If I go up to the heavens, you are there. If I rise on the wings of the dawn, if I settle on the far side of the sea, even there your hand will guide me, your right hand will hold me fast' (Ps. 139). God is all over the place. His presence is everywhere we go. If we recognized it more, we'd be tripping over him.

Some days we know that. Some of the time it's easy to feel God's presence really near, as if we could reach out and touch him. John Ortberg describes days like this as 'rainbow days'.[8] After God had brought Noah and his family safely through the flood in the ark, he said: 'This is the sign of the covenant I am making between me and you and every living creature with you, a covenant for all generations to come: I have set my rainbow in the clouds, and it

5. Esther de Waal, *Living with Contradiction: Benedictine wisdom for everyday living* (Canterbury Press, 2003), p. 101.

6. C.S. Lewis, *Letters to Malcolm: Chiefly on Prayer* (Harvest Books, 2002).

7. G.M. Hopkins, 'God's Grandeur', in D.H.S. Nicholson and A.H.E. Lee, *The Oxford Book of English Mystical Verse* (Clarendon Press, 1917).

8. Ortberg, *God is Closer than You Think*, p. 32.

will be the sign of the covenant between me and the earth' (Gen. 9.12–23). Every time Noah saw the rainbow, he remembered that God was with him.

Sometimes I have rainbow days too – when I just know God is with me. But a lot of the time my spiritual life is a bit routine. I settle in and I feel comfortable and perhaps I even get a little bit bored. In a sense there's nothing wrong with that. I became a Christian when I was seven. I hope to be a Christian all my life. My great-grandmother died when she was 103. Women in my family traditionally live for a long time. So I could be a Christian for 96 years! That's a marathon, not a sprint. If every day was a mountain top experience with God I would be exhausted. God is a natural, ordinary, comfortable part of my life.

So how do we follow a God who wants to be closer than our closest friend and so much part of our lives that there is nothing extraordinary about his presence – and also the God who wants us to grow, to stretch us, get to know us better and bring us life in all its fullness? How can we see the presence of God more in our everyday lives and hear his voice? How can we bring prayer into the everyday?

Perhaps we need to practise the way we pay attention to God, like we practise anything we want to get better at – like jogging or playing tennis or cooking. Maybe God is more present than we realize, but we just need to practise hearing his voice, which is sometimes a whisper. There is a book by a seventeenth-century monk named Brother Lawrence called *The Practice of the Presence of God*. He found that God's presence became very real to him the more he practised seeing God in the most mundane work: 'In continuing the practice of conversing with God throughout each day, and quickly seeking His forgiveness when I fell or strayed, His presence has become as easy and natural to me now as it once was difficult to attain.'[9]

God is already there, waiting for us. It is our task to live every day firmly rooted in his presence. Jean-Pierre de Caussade speaks

---

9. *The Practice of the Presence of God Brother Lawrence* (Hendrickson, 2004).

of 'the sacrament of the present moment'[10]. Each moment of every day is a means of grace and a vehicle for God's love and power. The statement 'Behold, I am making all things new' (Rev. 21.5) is not just a future promise but a statement about the continual renewing work of God in each moment of our lives, if we are open to it. Every situation, every relationship, brings us closer to divine grace, if we are ready to receive it. The Psalmist speaks of 'deep calling to deep'. That is what it is like when our innermost being calls to God's and back. Longing for God, listening for God, being in dialogue with God, is prayer. It does not always need a formal time or place. It can be part of everyday life and activity, as long as we try to be aware of it.

We tend to think of Moses' encounter with God in a burning bush (Exod. 3.1–6) as one of the Bible's 'earth-shattering events' which indeed it was. God revealed himself to Moses in a life-changing and history-making way. But it all started with something quite ordinary. It wasn't unusual that the bush was burning up. The desert was hot and things often caught fire. Moses could have seen the burning bush and thought, 'Oh look, a burning bush. How ordinary'. But what was not ordinary, and what Moses noticed, was that it wasn't burning up. So Moses 'turned aside' to see why. *Then* he experienced God being present in that place.

Moses might not have noticed. He might have gone on his way, his mind full of this and that. He might have thought: 'I haven't got the time. I've got so much to do. I'm so busy with these sheep.' But he didn't. He was alert and he experienced God in that ordinary bush that he may well have passed a hundred times before. In that moment the ordinary became extraordinary. But he first stopped and took notice.

Looking is different from seeing. It is seeing intently, purposefully, noticing. Moses said, 'I must *turn aside*.' Busy Christians need to master the art of 'turning aside' in the everyday whirl to see God. That might mean finding something familiar and really noticing what it is like, asking God to speak to you through it. A person (or your relationship with them); or the newspaper, or the

---

10. *The Sacrament of the Sacred Moment* (trans. Kitty Muggeridge; Harper San Francisco, 1989).

everyday things of your life – routines, travelling, work, preparing food, playing music, watching a film, looking at a view, a tree or a bunch of flowers. We see the nature of God in what he has made. He could have made one flower, but he made many. That shows us his generosity. He made small delicate birds. That shows his carefulness. He made mighty waves. That shows his power. He made the duck-billed platypus. That shows his sense of humour.

Sometimes God practically shouts at us through the things around us. The natural world has God's fingerprints all over it. Many scientists find themselves believing in God when they study the intricacies of the cosmos, or the human body or chemical structures, because there is too much that speaks of God to ignore. Rom. 1.20 says: 'For since the creation of the world his eternal power and divine nature, invisible though they are, have been made understood and seen through the things he has made. So they are without excuse'.

I don't think we need to fret about finding more time for extended periods of prayer and silence. What we do need is to incorporate prayer more into our everyday lives. I have heard of mothers who use the time when they're up in the small hours of the night feeding young babies to pray (those women must be saints). I know someone who uses the time after lunch when he takes the dog for a walk as a chance to reflect and pray. I know someone else who uses the long commute on the train to work as his prayer time. Far from being little moments we *add on* to our regular prayer life, whatever that might be, these regular but incorporated moments of the day can *become* our prayer life: 'All these short moments of prayer are moments of re-focusing. They are moments to recall God's presence. St Benedict's way to God does not live in any particular mystical experience, but in all the ordinariness of daily living.'[11]

Turning aside, looking with intent, is something we can do no matter how busy we get. In fact, the busier we are, the more opportunities we have to see God in all sorts of different and interesting places. Then, like Moses, we might find God saying to us too, 'take off the sandals from your feet, for the place on which

11. De Waal, *Living with Contradiction*, p. 105.

you are standing is holy ground'. The living-room, the kitchen, the office, the school run, the church – all is holy ground.

'The Bright Field' by R.S. Thomas expresses this need for seeing God in each precious moment:

> I have seen the sun break through
> to illuminate a small field
> for a while, and gone my way
> and forgotten it. But that was the pearl
> of great price, the one field that had
> treasure in it. I realize now
> that I must give all that I have
> to possess it. Life is not hurrying
> on to a receding future, nor hankering after
> an imagined past. It is the turning
> aside like Moses to the miracle
> of the lit bush, to a brightness
> that seemed as transitory as your youth
> once, but is the eternity that awaits you.[12]

Stepping above

So being busy and being prayerful need not exclude each other, contrary to what some might say. But each of us needs to find patterns and methods of prayer that are workable for our own individual lives and personalities. The way we choose to pray must be realistically achievable otherwise, like many a commitment to do more exercise, many a pledge to give up smoking and many a diet, it will simply fall by the wayside when the pressure sets in. We do long to be better and more prayerful Christians, but we've also got to be pragmatic and admit that if it's unrealistically demanding, or simply too difficult in our busy lives, we're liable to quit at the first hurdle. We don't like to own up to things like that. We'd rather say that we will strive to discipline ourselves to something

12. R.S. Thomas, *Collected Poems 1945–1990* (Phoenix Press, 2000).

better and higher, we'll try our hardest, inspired by the Holy Spirit – and all that. But we are human and we're fallible and we'll fail. So let's set the levels realistically and pray as we can, not as we can't, admitting that there's always room for improvement.

The patterns of prayer we set for ourselves, if they are nothing else, must be the following.

Sustainable (for the long haul)

We have already seen that prayer can be part of everyday life as we 'pray on the run', giving each situation to God as it arises, and hearing his voice in the everyday. However, there are also times when we need to *be sustained* in prayer, rather than being the ones doing the sustaining. That is where the corporate worship of the praying community, the Church, comes in.

Whatever tradition you worship in – high church and liturgical, or informal and spontaneous, those times of meeting with other Christians (all of whom struggle with prayer to some degree or other) are able to sustain you in your prayer life. One writer expresses how the words of the liturgy she prays on a Sunday sustain her 'praying on the go' from Monday to Saturday, as the words return to her in moments of busyness:

> The words of psalms and hymns and the lines from Scripture do not come out of thin air. They have been sown in my being across a lifetime of participation in public worship, study of the Bible, listening to sermons, reading devotional literature, Church history, and great literature, including poetry. God uses these resources, but also the other ingredients of our busy lives.[13]

It is not just we who sustain prayer, but prayer that sustains us.

13. Muriel Porter, 'Praying on the run – a spirituality for activists/extroverts', www.media.anglican.com.au.

Practical (in the everyday)

There is a need to find ways of praying that are practically attainable in the type of life you lead. It's no use saying you'll go to a monastery in the middle of nowhere once a month if you don't drive. There's no point committing to an hour's prayer first thing in the morning if you have a two-year old who likes to rise with the dawn. You might like to think about making a diary of what you do over a week, and working out from that how you might best pray. Be creative. Remember it's OK to pray while walking, while driving (if you remember to keep your eyes open), while hoovering, while working. Paul writes to the Ephesians: 'Pray all the time, asking for what you need' (Eph. 6.18).

I do quite a lot of walking around the city in which I live and I have begun to experiment with praying the Jesus Prayer[14] while walking. The Jesus Prayer is a simple prayer that comes out of the Eastern Orthodox tradition. Its words: 'Lord Jesus Christ, Son of God, have mercy on me, a sinner' are intended to be prayed repetitively, taking a breath in on the first part ('Lord Jesus Christ, Son of God') and a letting a breath out on the second ('have mercy on me, a sinner'). The intention is not to think too much about praying, but simply to allow the words, and the invocation of the name and the truth of Jesus to break through into your mind, your emotions and your soul. I find the rhythm of the prayer works well with the rhythm of walking. When I pray 'on the move', the things of the city – the cars, the people, the rubbish – seem to comment on my praying and vice versa. I get some funny looks when I realize I've been praying out loud, though.

Life-giving (relevant to all of your life)

Sometimes we have the idea that when we come to pray, we step out of the rest of our life and its concerns and into some holy and

14. For further reading, see, for example, Simon Barrington-Ward and Sister Theresa Margaret, *The Jesus Prayer* (BRF, 1996) and Brother Ramon and Simon Barrington-Ward, *Praying the Jesus Prayer Together* (BRF, 2004).

spiritual realm where we're only allowed to think 'religious thoughts'. God is interested in the whole of your life – so pray about the whole of your life. Break down the divide between the sacred and the secular, remembering the words of Brother Lawrence again: 'Whoever practises God's presence will soon become spiritual. How can we be with Him, unless our thoughts are with Him? How can He be in our thoughts unless we form a holy habit of abiding in His presence, there asking for the grace we need each moment of our life?'

Make a habit of praying about your life as you're living it. So as you put your kids to bed, be praying for them, maybe not in words out loud, but simply lifting them to God for his blessing. As you step into the office in the morning, commit that day to God and all it will hold, and so on.

Authentic (to who you are – your personality)

We're all different. Don't try to pray in the same way as another person you know, if that way doesn't feed your unique personality. I have found the personality indicators of Myers Briggs and Ennea-gram to be very helpful in working out what makes me tick. They don't put me in a box, but they do help me to have language to explain to myself and to others the way that I am. To give one example, extroverts in the Myers Briggs Personality Indicator get their energy from being with others. They process information best in dialogue, 'out there', rather than internally. If you are like this, you may find it easier to pray with others, rather than on your own. Don't be surprised if your prayer life with God becomes very much a dialogue between you and him. Find ways of praying that suit you.

Releasing (not guilt-inducing)

Don't feel guilty about prayer. Like everything in life, long to do it better, but start from where you are.

God is waiting to meet you there...

Busy building the kingdom 5

When Jesus left the earth, he didn't say, 'Put your feet up and have a rest'. He didn't say, 'It's OK. Leave it all to me. I'll manage on my own'. He said: 'All authority in heaven and on earth has been given to me. Go therefore and make disciples of all nations, baptizing them in the name of the Father and of the Son and of the Holy Spirit, and teaching them to obey everything that I have commanded you' (Mt. 28.18).

If we are to fulfil Jesus's great commission, we're going to be working hard. If we take seriously Jesus's imperative to bring the Gospel to every man and woman and child in a way that is as compelling and exciting as its source and author, we're going to be doing more than sitting around contemplating our navels. For good or ill, the main vehicle of bringing the Gospel to people today is the church, which is the subject of this chapter.

Being the church today, doing the things that Jesus asks us to do, is a demanding and energetic task. Yes, he uses us in our brokenness and weakness, as he was weak and broken, but it is through ordinary Christians that he chooses to fulfil his work in the world. The good news is that Jesus doesn't leave us to do it alone. The next bit of that quotation from Matthew ch. 28 says: 'And remember, I am with you always, to the end of the age.'

There is a balance to be had between being active in what we do as Christians and as churches, and being fully reliant on God and eager to deepen our relationship, both individual and corporate, with him. As churches, we will need to be busy if we are to survive at all, but we will need to learn to listen to God if we are to survive as Christians and as people.

David Runcorn puts it like this:

There are perils as well as opportunities in reaching out to the weary hedonism of our age. Vital though it is to be developing strategies for transforming church life, ministry and mission, Christian living can easily become little more than a religious version of the anxious restlessness around us. ... We offer a frantic spirituality for a frantic age. And what do we gain if we fill the whole church and lose our soul?[1]

Could it be that church has become just another source of stress, busyness and 'anxious restlessness' for Christians?

Church, and the commitment it demands, has become for some people another burden on an already hectic life. There are many people in the church I go to who have very busy lives. They are doctors, accountants, hospital workers, fathers, mothers, grand-parents. They do football coaching and lead Scouts and are parent governors at their kids' schools. Church is just one of the things they fit into their Sundays. There are children to get to football practice, meals to be had with friends and relatives, homework to be completed (for adults and children) and shopping to be done. In today's increasingly mobile society, many people go away for weekends to visit friends and relatives. Some of the most com-mitted people now come to church, not every week, but every fortnight or so. This is not lack of devotion. It is not backsliding. It is not a sign of increasing heathen-ness. It is a sign of a busy life and it is reality.

So why is church so busy these days? How can church become again the revitalizing, refreshing community it is meant to be, where we are resourced for all of life, rather than being drained of any energy we have left in our already stretched resources? These are big questions. But if church is not a meeting but a body, not an institution but a family, not a club but a community, we have to ask questions about what part exactly church activities play in our lives. If there is no divide between sacred and secular, then all time and everything we do is 'of God' and in God, and that includes church.

There are several immediately identifiable reasons for the increase in activity and busyness in many churches – and some that are not quite as obvious.

1. David Runcorn, *Choice, Desire and the Will of God* (SPCK, 2003), p. 115.

Messages

Church is becoming more professional

When I say the church is becoming more professional, I don't mean that it is being staffed by more paid workers. Quite the opposite. In some areas those being paid for the ministry they do are few and far between. What I mean is that what the church is doing is generally being done better (with some increasingly glaring exceptions).

The old assumptions that Britain is a Christian country, that every person living in a geographical radius around a church is a parishioner and that the church just needs to keep on ticking over, just don't wash any more. Declining church attendance and changing patterns in society mean that the Church has got to radically re-imagine how it does things.

In reaching out to a generation used to professionalism in all areas of life, the Church needs to match the high standards it sees all around it. More and more churches are endeavouring to present a good image to those they come into contact with and to advertise rather than just exist. So notice-boards are professionally designed, music is led by trained musicians, youth work done by paid youth workers and impressive projection systems installed. This is not a bad thing. The Church has too often been seen as amateurish and unattractive. The Gospel of Jesus Christ is and always has been something that offers freedom and fulfilment, but we haven't always presented it this way.

As well as doing what we've always done well better, we now have to think of different ways of doing things too. So we have evangelism initiatives, discipleship courses, church growth projects, buildings reordered and improved for use by the local community, changes in the way we do worship, changes in the way we do mission and changes in the way we offer practical care. In many churches there has been a proliferation in the range and type of activities offered. And they all need people to run them.

The Church in Britain is in a time of newness. There is a great excitement around about the opportunities today's post-modern, post-Christian, spiritually-aware society presents in terms of evangelism and church growth. But there is also an awareness that it won't happen by standing still.

Every member ministry is hard work

The days are gone (thank goodness) when you could leave it all to the vicar. A reduction in the number of paid clergy means that more lay people are doing things the vicar used to do. The task of ministry is increasingly being carried out in teams, lay and ordained. This is excellent. No one ever said ministry was meant to be a one-man show. But the development of good, working teams means there is more to be done by people other than the clergy, and so church life gets busier for those involved.

The danger comes when the 'more' there is to be done is done by fewer people. It is popularly estimated that 80 per cent of the work in churches is done by 20 per cent of the people. So it becomes not 'every member ministry', but the ministry of the few very committed. The adage that if you want something doing, ask a busy person, certainly seems to be true in the life of the church. But it's not healthy, for the people involved, or for the church, for a few people to be doing all the work. The challenge for many churches is to encourage *all* of the church members to play their part in building God's kingdom, both in church life and in other areas of everyday living.

Great expectations

Sometimes we have to step back and ask ourselves, why am I doing this? What is my motivation for all this activity? Is it because it is my God-given calling to fulfil this task or that, or am I simply trying to fulfil other people's expectations of me? This is no less true when it comes to what we are doing (or not doing) in church.

There are many motivations for being busy at church, and not all of them are good, for either ourselves or the church we're involved with. There are certain features of our psychological make-up which if not watched and checked have the potential to add to over-busyness and burnout. Some of these features are true for many people – lay and ordained – but I think they have particular resonance for clergy and church leaders.

Low self-esteem is a problem for clergy on whom expectations are placed that are at best difficult and at worst impossible to fulfil. For women clergy, the problem may be doubly real. Lucy Winkett (who has been a role model for many women clergy, as the first woman staff member at St Paul's Cathedral) expresses this: 'The pressure of fulfilling dual roles of public priest and domestic goddess meet in the lives of women clergy: we not only open the fête; we are also asked to bake a cake for the mothers' union stall.'[2]

No clergyperson or layperson, male or female, can ever live up to all the expectations placed upon them. Often we find ourselves out of breath because of the unrealistic expectations we have of ourselves, the desire to feel important and needed, and the need for security. This can apply to churches as a whole as well as individual members. The need is to keep a check on our motivations, and to make sure we are doing what God is calling us to do – no more and no less – in the knowledge that our security and identity is found in him.

Being perfect

Sometimes we take on too much as churches and as individuals because of a drive for perfection.

I have felt this very keenly. I am someone who loves to do well at everything. I have never found failure of any kind easy. I find it hard to give less than 100 per cent, but sometimes there isn't time for 100 per cent, there's only time for 99.9 per cent. I know I feel the pressure to be as good as I can possibly be, not just because I want to, or because I'm a perfectionist, but because I know people will be watching me to see how well I do things – as a woman. Being an advertisement for any type, for women clergy, for

2. Lucy Winkett, *Church Times*, 12 March 2004.

women, for clergy, for church wardens, for worship leaders, for Christians, can be a very heavy burden to carry.

The drive for excellence is not a bad thing, and I have already spoken about the need to say 'yes' as well as 'no'. Indeed we should give all that we can to the work of God and do everything to the best of our ability. However, the drive for unattainable perfection is exhausting and is liable to lead to burnout.

Pleasing everyone

Too often, we take things upon ourselves to make sure that everyone is happy. We cave in to feelings of guilt: 'What kind of awful person am I not to offer my help? I really have no choice but to do this.' So in churches up and down the land there are church leaders bending over backwards to incorporate and accommodate the differing worship tastes of their congregations, as well as reaching out to those outside the church. It is never possible to be accepted by everyone, and the compulsion to please has a tendency to lead to exhaustion, as we take on more and more activities in order to keep everyone happy.

Many women, particularly, feel a strong need to be accepted by others, linked perhaps to a concern for relationships. A woman may have been encouraged through her life experiences to make herself acceptable to others, especially men. A fear of 'rocking the boat' might account for some of the fiercest opposition to women's ordination coming from other women. Women have often colluded with the stereotypes of them because it feels safer. There is a fear of stridency and of ceasing to be appealingly 'feminine'.

Constantly wanting to make oneself acceptable can also lead to an inability to deal with conflict and a shying away from divisive issues. It might lead to an avoidance of offering vision in leadership, or at least any vision with which one suspects all might not agree. Penny Jamieson, the first female bishop, argues against a misguided use of the concept of 'acceptance' for women in ministry in particular, because it leads to a blunting of their prophetic and gospel ministry in the world: 'I would not like to see the ministry of women hamstrung by an over-dependence on acceptance at the expense of clarity about the Christ they serve.'[3] For women leaders, the realization that we cannot please everyone all the time leads to a greater ability to face conflict constructively and lead communities forward in vision.

The tendency to seek acceptance is by no means limited to women or to leaders, but may be felt all the more keenly by them.

The need to be needed

We may choose to do tasks in church because we want to feel needed, imagining that the more we do the better others will view us.

We need to learn to include ourselves as *part* of any solution, alongside others. This might mean taking more time to care for our own needs, rather than constantly considering only the needs of those we serve. Not until a person has a strong sense of their own worth in God's eyes is she or he able truly to communicate a sense of worth to others. The Christian philosophy of 'denying oneself' is a virtuous way of living, but until we learn to take care of ourselves as well, we are not truly mature and responsible people.

Many women in particular find it difficult to foster a healthy sense of self-esteem, perhaps due to the expectations placed upon them by stereotypes of care and self-giving. Studies consistently speak of women's low self-esteem. In one study of 1,300 students at Bible college, 31 per cent of women said they had above average competence compared to 70 per cent of men, while 51 per cent of women at mainstream universities and 58 per cent of men said they had above average competence.[4] Nurturing women's feelings of self-worth is perhaps one of the fundamental tasks facing the Church and those who care for its leaders.

3. Penny Jamieson, *Living at the Edge: Sacrament and solidarity in leadership* (Mowbray, 1997), p. 135.
4. Cited in G. Troup, 'Women's Work', article in *Idea*, the magazine of the Evangelical Alliance, January–March 1999: 21–23.

A life of service

Christians are called to a life of service, but service that flows out of a healthy relationship with God and a strong regard for our own well-being and wholeness. Only this type of service is 'perfect freedom'. Service that springs from any other motivation is wrought with problems.

Of course, the model of service is a fundamental tenet of the call of Christ, and is crucial to the very nature of discipleship, stemming from the life of Christ and his sacrifice. However, in the past, service has often been the *only* model presented to Christians, especially women. Other important facets of the Christian life, like authority, power and vision, have been ignored.

Pamela Evans, in her excellent book on Christians avoiding burnout, says: 'Those who serve in order to find the significance they feel they lack, or to earn God's favour, will serve with a determination brought about by fear and uncertainty.'[5]

A survey amongst male and female ordinands training for ministry at theological college listed a number of possible elements associated with ordained ministry and asked: 'Which elements appeal to you most?' More women chose 'care' (seven women compared with three men) and 'service' (eight women compared with three men) as the most appealing elements in ministry for them. More men than women stressed 'vision' (nine men compared with three women), 'leadership' (seven men compared with three women) and 'authority' (two men compared with one woman) as the most appealing elements.

Whilst being a worthy model for ministry of any kind, ordained or lay, 'serving' can also be a cover for feelings of worthlessness, especially in women. When a woman's life is predominantly shaped by caring and she receives affirmation only through this channel, then she will naturally seek affirmation in *whichever* sphere she operates by taking care of others, as she has done as a mother or in similar roles. Although this concern for relationship is undoubtedly a good and honourable part of women's make-up, it has a negative side. Alongside it, women are often given the subconscious message

---

5. Pamela Evans, *Driven Beyond the Call of God* (Oxford, Bible Reading Fellowship, 1999), p. 169.

that self-serving will destroy harmony and that the pursuit of one's own needs is selfish. As with all theologies, a theology of service can be used to build people up and to find wholeness through Christ, or it can be used to keep people in their place.

Again, the problem of self-sacrifice becoming oppression is doubly present for clergy. For too long clergy have interpreted the call to 'laying down their lives' in the same way Jesus did, as synonymous with being constantly available. For some church leaders this has led to a difficulty in drawing healthy boundaries around different aspects of life – ministry, family, leisure and rest. Stress and burnout has often been the result.

A godly perspective

We have seen some of the motivations for busyness in church life, which tend to lead to more pressure and add to the stress. However, the church at the moment is also an exciting place in a new phase of opportunity. What did God *really* intend for his people together?

Church as community

Community is one of the best answers to the issue of busyness and pressure in the church that I know. Not that living in community makes it all OK, but there are certain things that happen in community – real community worked out and lived out – that might help with our current anxieties about how to function as a church of busy, stressed-out people. If we see church not as a place, or an activity, but as a community, it makes it a lot easier to imagine creative ways in which this community, or family, might meet together in ways that are healthy, life-giving and attractive.

The Greek word for church is 'ekklesia', meaning 'called out'. It is not a noun, but a verb. People can be 'called out' in whatever expression church takes – a midweek prayer time, an alternative worship community, a home group, a women's breakfast, the whole of life.

There are things to be learned from the way in which the first Christians met together when we're looking at building community in the modern church. The first church existed and grew in very different circumstances to the ones we find ourselves in today. First-century Jerusalem is a very different place from twenty-first century Bristol – different place, different time, different culture, different values, different society, different people. But the same God.

There is a lovely verse describing the Church in Acts 9.31: 'Meanwhile the Church throughout Judea, Galilee, and Samaria had peace and was built up. Living in the fear of the Lord and in the comfort of the Holy Spirit, it increased in numbers.' One of the defining qualities of the early church as described in the book of Acts was that they were a real and authentic community. They seemed to have a quality of living and being together that meant that the church was strong and more people wanted to join it.

People today still want to belong to something. If the church is to be a place that is attractive and refreshing for ordinary, busy people, we need to rediscover a real sense of community authentic to our culture. Community at its best is the place where we can bring everything we are, and all our busyness, to be together with other people who know and accept us. If this sounds like a utopian dream, then think again. God's intention from the beginning of time is that people should live together, with God, in community. Dallas Willard said: 'God's aim in human history is the creation of an inclusive community of loving persons, with himself included as its primary sustainer and most glorious inhabitant.'[6]

Meeting together

Our world is becoming a society of dis-connection, where people often don't want to meet with others, or certainly not with others

6. Quoted in John Ortberg, *Everybody's Normal Till You Get to Know Them* (Zondervan, 2003).

who are not of their own choosing. Fewer and fewer people are choosing to mix with people who are not 'like them' in some way. People do yearn for community, but mostly those are made up of 'people like me'. An advert for joining a web-based blog community announced 'Meet people like you'. You don't have to meet anyone at the shops, because you can do it all over the Internet, you don't even have to meet anyone to go to church, because you can join a 'virtual' church. I was amused to read that a new web-based cyber-church is running into the same problems as ordinary physical ones. The world's first Internet church, run by the Ship of Fools website,[7] has been attacked by cyber demons – particularly from Australia and the USA–logging on as Satan. The church had to restrict access to areas such as the altar and pulpit and struggled to develop security to rid the blasphemers from their midst: 'A spokesman said they were looking for more money so they can employ wardens around the clock.' Wardens – that'll sort them out.

The earliest believers built community by meeting together, bodily, in the same place at the same time. They weren't just some loose affiliation of people interested in the same thing. Acts 2.46 tells us they met together every day in the temple, and in their homes. Physically meeting together must be important because when it looked as if they might stop doing it, they were challenged: 'And let us consider how to provoke one another to love and good deeds, not neglecting to meet together, as is the habit of some, but encouraging one another, and all the more as you see the Day approaching' (Heb. 10.24–25).

One of the challenges facing the Church today is to work out what kind of meeting together builds community today. We have already said that people struggle to come to church every week. Our busy, full and dispersed lives mean that weekly gathering might be the ideal but is often not the reality. Can we find ways of meeting together that are more accessible, and that are enriching for those involved?

The report *Churchgoing Today* says 'modern-day weekends are full with domestic and personal agendas that combine to mean that

---

7. www.shipoffools.com.

Sunday services present difficult choices for many ... We need to give permission to put energy into providing opportunities for worship that accommodate the different lifestyles in our neighbourhood.'[8] So one church in an area where many children play football on a Sunday morning puts on a Sunday teatime service (with tea and cakes) for the children and their parents. There are churches that have their main meeting midweek, including one in Bristol that gathers in a coffee bar. What might it look like in your context?

Unity in diversity

The Church in Acts was made up of people who would never, humanly speaking, dream of meeting together. There was an astonishing racial and cultural mix. It would have been unheard of for a slave-owner and his slave to be together in any other context, but the letter of Paul to Philemon is written to a slave-owner, asking him to accept his runaway slave, Onesimus, as a brother in Christ. Samaritans and Jews met together, as did Jews and Gentiles. These kinds of relationships would have been impossible in any other setting because of the hatred and suspicion that existed between them. But amazingly they met in Christian fellowship, such that Paul is able to write in Col. 3.11: 'there is no longer Greek and Jew, circumcised and uncircumcised, barbarian, Scythian, slave and free; but Christ is all and in all!'

The community at Lee Abbey is made up of people from 20 different nationalities. People are drawn to the community from different countries, ethnic groups, denominations and political persuasions, which is not without its challenges. It doesn't mean that differences are glossed over, or that everyone must be 'the same'. The differences are celebrated as part of community living. There have been occasions where community members from one church tradition have had to learn to live and worship alongside people from entirely different traditions (strongly protestant French

8. Lynda Barley, Head of Research and Statistics for the Archbishops' Council, *Time to Listen: Churchgoing Today* (Church House Publishing, 2006).

Baptist with Romanian Roman Catholic, for example). This has often been an enriching experience on both sides as people learn to see relationships with people rather than denominational dogma as the important thing, and to receive from each other's traditions.

In a very real way there *is* male and female, slave and free, Jew and Greek. There *are* different ages, different genders, different backgrounds, different tastes in worship style in many churches. The important thing is that we can be different and yet meet together in fellowship and worship.

One area where this is particularly seen is in the collaboration between men and women. At Lee Abbey both men and women are chaplains and worship leaders, preachers and presidents. It has not always been the case, but gender equality is now a key feature of the ministry. Several people have commented that the issues surrounding the ordination of women that seemed so important in their home churches grow less significant in the context of an open and loving community where people are known and valued for who they are in Christ and given roles according to gifting rather than gender. It is entirely plausible (indeed it has happened) at Lee Abbey that a service might be led by a female president, with a female preacher and music leader, with an all-male dance group performing a worship dance – and for this to happen without special comment! The community has come to accept the normality of men and women working together in whatever role God has given them, such that it has become unremarkable, yet it remains a witness to the wider Church.[9]

There will be other barriers that can, and need to be, broken down in the context of worship – old and young, able-bodied and those with special needs, for instance. Barriers are broken down as people learn to live and worship together. But that might involve making sacrifices – by women, by men, by everyone, as we shall see.

9. For a fuller discussion of these themes, see Chris Edmondson and Emma Ineson, *Celebrating Community: God's gift for today's world* (Darton, Longman and Todd, 2006).

Partnership and sacrifice

Being together is not easy. The one thing we definitely have in common is that we are all human, and we all have weaknesses and imperfections. None of us is perfect. Henri Nouwen has said: 'We are unified by our common weaknesses, our common failures, our common disappointments and our common inconsistencies.'[10] One of the areas of weakness that comes to the fore very often in the Church is in the relating between men and women, between sexuality and gender, most often at an institutional level.

Partnership

The premise of this book, that increased communication and partnership between men and women will lead to a healthier way of life for both, is particularly salient in relation to the life of the Church. If the ideal Christian community is one in which there is no male nor female, slave nor free but all are one in Christ Jesus, how does this translate into today's church life? Is the church a place where the gifts of both men and women can be used to the full, so that the life of the Church is enriched and renewed for all?

Is church good for men?

On the one hand some men are saying they've had enough. There has been a recent rise in the number of publications and organizations declaring that Church as it is at the moment doesn't work for men, that's it's too 'feminine' and something needs to change to make church more 'man-friendly'. Organizations like 'Geezers for Jesus'[11] state that 'church can be a very feminine place, and some guys feel emasculated'. Dave Murrrow[12], an American writer, claims that the emotive worship, inclusive language and a

10. Henri Nouwen, *Reaching Out* (Zondervan, 1998).
11. www.geezersforjesus.co.uk.
12. Author of *Why Men Hate Going to Church* (Nelson Books, 2005).

lack of 'masculine' culture in the Church is leading to a 'feminization' that excludes men (despite the fact that 95 per cent of senior pastors in the United Sates are male). He advocates male leadership (on the basis that 'women will follow a man, but few men will follow a woman'), increased emphasis on God as Father, a rediscovery of 'Christ the man' ('Wildman, King, Son, Warrior, Judge and Brother'), meeting outdoors for worship, charging men for church-based activities ('men equate money with value') and the creation of a 'masculine' environment as a means of getting men back into church. Murrow claims: 'We don't have to have hand-to-hand combat during the worship service to get men there. We just have to start speaking [their language], use the metaphors they understand and create an environment that feels masculine to them.'

Maybe the Church does need to attract more men, but making the Church more 'masculine' might not be the answer. Neither will making the Church more 'feminine' attract more women. The Church is made up of both men and women who would do well to seek to understand their similarities as well as their differences and together to seek a God who is neither male nor female, but who makes both in God's image.

One of the big assumptions behind the 'church is no good for men argument' is that church is only any good as long as it is meeting *my* needs, as long as it is doing things I like the way *I* like them. It's a consumer model of church. The Church is not the institution. The Church is not the leaders. The Church is you. And me. So if there are things to change about the Church it is up to all of us, men and women, ordained and lay, to change them together, but with respect, admiration and hospitality towards the gifts and abilities of every individual person, whatever their gender.

Is church good for women?

For men and women to work together in an institution in which men have held most of the power for the past 2,000 years is not easy. For many years, the Church has not been a place that encourages and nurtures the gifts of women, especially in leadership, despite what Murrow maintains about it being 'too feminine'. In the Church of England, at least, much has improved over the past 12 years since the admission of women to the priesthood. But there is still a long way to go: 2000 years of patriarchy in church life and structures is going to take a long time to balance out.

I vividly recall, as a curate in Sheffield, going to visit the family of a man who had died and whose funeral I was to take. The man's wife welcomed me and we had a good conversation about how she would like the funeral to go. Halfway through the visit, the couple's son, a brusque Yorkshireman, arrived at the house. He came through the door and I rose to shake his hand. He took one look at me in my dog-collar and, keeping his hand firmly by his side, said simply, 'I don't think Father would approve of *that*'. Those two reactions, of welcome and appreciation of my ministry by his wife, and of rude dismissiveness by his son, epitomized for me the attitudes towards women in ministry that still exist in the Church today.

The Church is becoming increasingly welcoming of the gifts and ministries of women in all areas of the Church. Women are coming into a time of unparalleled opportunity, in service and in leadership and in transforming both. In doing so, women can claim and own all the qualities and characteristics needed to minister effectively, without fearing being seen as 'unfeminine'. Once we take on the mantle of a fully sanctioned and autonomous authority, we can reject the label 'unfeminine', just as we can reject the accusation that the Church is 'unmasculine'.

Women are called upon to take our rightful place alongside men at the altar, in the crèche, in the music group, on the tea rota, and in every aspect of ministry, taking responsibility seriously, transforming power, enabling others and rediscovering self-esteem in the process. The way forward is for male and female to be what God has called them to be together, not bound by restrictive patterns. It is for women to reject false stereotypes that have constrained them in the past; to reserve for themselves the freedom to be fully human. Most of all it is in the embracing of the fact that we are made in God's image as women and as men.

Being part of a church that is still not sure about the ministry of women in all areas of church life, as well as being unsure about how best to welcome men, is going to involve surrendering some things that have long been held dear, by men and by women. Being a real community will involve sacrifice, on the part of men, of women and of everyone.

Sacrifice

Sacrificing time 'doing something else' in favour of meeting with other Christians

Church is never going to fit into busy lives. Perhaps it's not about making church 'fit', but a complete sea change in attitude, where our everyday lives *are* church (in the sense that they're lived out in the presence of God) and meeting with other Christians is a natural part of that lived experience. If we begin to see church as community, as family, as brothers and sisters in Christ, then the desire to meet with fellow Christians will follow from there. As with anything else in the busyness, if it is a priority for you, you'll make time for it, maybe at the expense of other activities.

Sacrificing individuality in favour of community

In the same way that you don't choose your family, you don't choose the person worshipping in the pew next to you. That means it's not always going to be all sweetness and light. Building real community takes time, effort, commitment and surrender. It means laying down some of my rights as an individual for the good of the body.

In the community at Lee Abbey there were several people whom I did not like very much. We differed in temperament, in political persuasion, in theology, in interests, in the way we did things. We would not dream of being together in any sphere otherwise, except that we were members of the same community, brothers and sisters in Christ, and that is what drew us together. The conflict that inevitably ensues when normal, flawed human beings live in community with other normal, flawed human beings can be creative and rewarding if faced and addressed in the love of

God. Jean Vanier, who founded the l'Arche communities, says this: 'Communities need tensions if they are to grow and deepen. Tensions come from conflicts ... a tension or difficulty can signal the approach of a new grace of God. But it has to be looked at wisely and humanly.'[13]

If church is community, or family, it's not about always getting your own way, or doing things the way you like it: 'Church as family is primarily about relationships. It is not about meetings, events or structures ... People are part of a kingdom community even if they don't get their needs met and often whether they feel like it or not.'[14] St Paul put it like this: 'Do nothing from selfish ambition or conceit, but in humility regard others as better than yourselves. Let each of you look not to your own interests, but to the interests of others' (Phil. 2.3–4).

It is impossible to plan worship, or church events, or an ethos in church life that everyone will love all the time (I know, I've tried). Where we work together with others, there will be sacrifices of our own personal taste in favour of what we know will bless others. Doing action songs might not be my preferred way of worshipping, but if I know the four-year-old beside me is getting a lot out of it, then I'll rejoice and have a go. A bit later in the service, my four-year-old friend might have to be patient with me as we sit and pray quietly for a while. Singing songs that are more 'feminine' (as some might have it) in tone might not be what the man next to me would prefer to sing, but if he knows it is helping the woman next to him to meet with God that morning, then he'll give it a go. And the woman next to him will be patient when some later element of the service appeals more to the man's sensibilities than to her own. Learning tolerance and sacrifice is a lesson much needed in the Body of Christ.

It is important to remember that the Christian community is a waiting community, that is, a community which not only creates a sense of belonging, but also a sense of estrangement. In

---

13. Jean Vanier, *Community and Growth* (Darton, Longman and Todd, 1989).

14. Eddie Gibbs and Ryan Bolger, *Emerging Churches: Creating Christian Communities in Postmodern Cultures* (SPCK, 2006), p. 97.

the Christian community, we say to each other We are together, but we cannot fulfil each other, we help each other, but
we also have to remind each other that our destiny is beyond
our togetherness. There is a constant encouragement to look
forward to what is to come.[15]

Sacrificing 'rights' as men and as women in favour of responsibilities to each other

Whilst many men rejoice at the recognition of women's priesthood and enjoy the fact that women have found a valid place in all
areas of the Church, including in its leadership, there are still some
who do not feel so positive. There are still some women who feel
as though they are working against a 'brotherhood'. For some male
clergy, being part of an all-male club held a great deal of appeal and
they feel the loss of the 'old boys' network'.

Sue Walrond-Skinner speaks of the sense of invasion felt by some
male clergy who have had a monopoly on the 'feminine' gifts of
intuition, compassion and teamwork.[16] Now that there are 'real'
women ministering alongside men, what will happen to the pastoral
ministry of men? The change that the ordination of women has
brought to male clergy identity at emotional and psychological
levels must not be underestimated. Whilst feeling at one level
completely happy with women's ministry, there might be more
deeply perceived threats, not least because of current confusions and
contradictions about what it means to be a man in today's society.

There may be things women also need to consider now. We
may need to listen to the voices saying that the Church is not good
for men. Although I don't agree with some of the foundational
ideas on which the views are based, I still need to listen to what is
being said out of respect for my brothers in Christ and a desire to
see them grow in their faith. So I may need to find ways of helping
church to be more welcoming to the average 'man on the street'
and to lay down some of my own preferences in the process.

15. Nouwen, *Reaching Out*, p. 119.
16. Sue Walrond-Skinner, *Double Blessing* (Mowbray, 1989), p. 37.

Stepping above

I'd like to suggest one or two changes that might make it easier to be a busy Christian involved in church life today.

Be positive about the local church

The world is changing and the Church must change too. In a world in which people are very open spiritually but often don't connect this with organized religion, there are vast opportunities for change and growth. And this is going to take some hard work. However, instead of feeling burdened by an ever-increasing task, adding to our ever-increasing busyness, the challenge is for those involved with the local church to start to radically re-imagine the way things *could* be. This will involve the changes in attitude we have addressed in this chapter.

How do we hold together the awful headlines about the Church, 'Bishops warn that "Church could disappear" within 50 years',[17] with the fact that Jesus said, 'And I tell you, you are Peter, and on this rock I will build my church, and the gates of Hades will not prevail against it' (Mt. 16.18)?

It is easy to get depressed about the state of the Church, but it is still the way in which God chooses to reach this world. The Church will never be perfect. There is a saying that if you find the perfect church you shouldn't join it in case you spoil it. Of course things could always improve, but we have no choice but to start with what we've got. Making any expression of church the best it can be takes prayer, submission and love for the Body of Christ – warts and all.

Perhaps we need to each ask ourselves whether we have a 'glass half full' or a 'glass half empty' attitude to the Church. One day, when Mat and I were exploring our callings to our curacy post, we went to see someone connected with the diocese in which we were hoping to work. The meeting was intended to be a chance

---

17. *Church of England Newspaper*, 25 March 2004.

for us to talk with this older, more mature clergyman who had been in ministry for many years about the realities and opportunities of our doing the curacy as a job-share. It was the most depressing meeting we have ever had. Not only did this man put a huge damper on the possibility that a job-share could ever be anything other than a consummate disaster for Mat, myself, our children, the church and the entire kingdom of God, he was also hugely gloomy about the Church in general. He told us about the negative effect being in ministry had had on his family and on his whole life. We felt sorry for him, ignored most of what he said and went on to a very fulfilling, enjoyable and successful job-share curacy.

I love the Church. Even more strangely, I love the Church of England. It's good to be positive about whatever church or denomination you belong to. And if you don't agree with something you see happening there – become a part of changing it. The answer is not to be grinning while it all falls apart around you, but being realistically positive and enthusiastic about the Church which is nothing less than Christ's body on this earth.

Do an audit of what you are doing in church

Soon after we were married, Mat and I were involved in an active, professional, lively church in Birmingham. It was the place where we met, it had become our spiritual home and we were a part of the community. We ended up saying 'yes' to doing so many things that there was virtually nothing that between the two of us we weren't involved in. Mat was on the PCC. I ran a Sunday school group. We led a home group. I helped plan all-age services. Mat played in the worship band. And so on. One day our vicar came to us and said, 'We really need some people to lead the youth group. They've been through a steady succession of leaders and they need someone who'll take it on and stay committed to the work. I'd love you to do it.' Our first reaction was that we couldn't possibly do that on top of everything else. But he went on, 'So I'd like you to give up everything else you're doing and just concentrate on the youth work.' We knew he was right. We had both known for a while that our growing passion was to work with young people (we were already helping on a summer youth camp) and that leading the youth group was exactly what we should be doing at this time. But nothing else. And so we did it. Other people were found to do the things we'd been doing and we spent several very happy years totally committed to that group of young people.

Should you be doing less? Should you be doing more? Should you be saying 'no' more? Should you be saying 'yes' more? Should you be focusing more on another aspect of your life – your work, your family, for instance? Are you constrained by wrong expectations put on you on the basis of gender? These are some of the questions you might ask yourself, prayerfully, and with the help and guidance of other mature Christians, in order to discern what your role in the body of Christ should be.

Examine your motivations for ministry

Why do you do what you do at church? When church begins to feel more like a burden and less like a blessing, perhaps that's when we need to start asking the big questions about what it's for, what is our part in it, and what we are doing it for anyway.

We have already seen how a lot of church activity has the potential to be motivated by issues arising out of a lack of secure identity. But the process of asking the questions is a healthy one which could lead to being released from pressures of expectation, image and unattainable standards. The answers to some of those questions might not be easy to deal with. Perhaps get someone else to do the asking with you, and pray with you about the outcomes.

Find your passion

If you are busy, you can't do everything. So deciding what you should be doing in the Church is the first step. Find what your passion is and use that in God's service. The Olympic runner Eric

Liddell, about whom the film *Chariots of Fire* was made, said this: 'I believe God made me for a purpose, but he also made me fast. And when I run I feel His pleasure.' What is it you do that instils in you a sense of God's pleasure? What were you made to do?

Again, in exploring what we are called to do or not do in church life, it is about calling and vocation. One of the tools I have found most helpful in this process both for myself and with others is the SHAPE questionnaire.[18] SHAPE stands for **S**piritual gifts, **H**eart, **A**bilities, **P**ersonality and **E**xperiences. It is a tool to help you to analyse the whole of your life, not just the more obviously 'spiritual' bits, in order to discern what your gifts, skills and passions might be – and how you might use them in the life of the Church.

Tools such as these might give you some indication of the kind of ministry you could be involved in at your church – and therefore the kinds of ministries you should *not* be involved in. For some people that might mean stopping what you are currently doing. It might mean taking up something new. It might mean stopping doing any ministry at all in church in order to be able to concentrate time and effort elsewhere. If your church has a good perspective on whole-life discipleship, it should be able to handle that! I know people who could be involved in many ministries at church because they're talented, resourceful people, but actually they are more effective if they're released to do what they're good at in the world.

Take seriously the call to community

Consumer culture says you only stay in church as long as you are getting your needs met. So when you get really busy, you stop being committed. Christians who take the call to community seriously recognize that even if it's not convenient, or going well or enjoyable, church is still where they belong because of the

18. See, for example, the Network course by Bruce Bugbee, Don Cousins, Bill Hybels and Wendy Seidman, produced by the Willow Creek Association and Bruce Bugbee, *Discover Your Spiritual Gifts the Network Way* (Zondervan, 2005).

community of relationships they are committed to, not least with God.

No one ever said this would be easy, but becoming authentic communities of growth, which are attractive and sustainable and refreshing, is a key issue for today's Church.

> Creating a vital community is a challenge in our current cultural context. People are both hungry for relationships and yet at the same time ill prepared for the costs involved. In a culture in which casual relationships and contractual relationships are the norm, it is difficult to build relationships based on deep foundations that can survive disagreements and disappointments. People are more prone to walk away when the going becomes difficult than to work through a crisis to the point where a new depth of understanding is reached.[19]

The challenge is to model something different, even when busy.

Be part of developing a real partnership between men and women

It is erroneous to think of any gifts as being inherently 'masculine' or 'feminine' or for either sex to have a monopoly on pastoring or caring or leading or taking authority or anything else. The only thing men or women in church have to fear is stereotyping. Women and men need be sensitive to each other's needs and fears, especially while both are coming to terms with the changes women's ordination brings. Women might be accepted into increasingly more responsible positions in the Church, but old attitudes are difficult to change, and take time to do so. It may take some sacrifices on both 'sides'. The Church must not be 'dominated by men' nor 'taken over by women'.

What is needed is a move away from inflexibly attaching any particular *quality* to men or to women uniquely; detaching characteristic from gender; removing gifts or callings from the terms

19. Gibbs and Bolger, *Emerging Churches*, p. 97.

'masculine' and 'feminine'; removing the labels 'male-friendly' or 'female-friendly' from any particular style of worship or way of doing church; and certainly stopping referring to the 'feminization' or the 'masculinity' of the Church.

Another step precedes all this – our conceptualization of God must be unhooked from its links with sexuality. One of the greatest dangers for men or for women is to see God as literally male. We must use language with care. 'Father' is a useful metaphor for God, but it is exactly that – a metaphor. God is not male and neither is God female. So it's OK for men to sing love songs to God and it's OK for women to offer the invitation of Christ at the altar.

The presence of women and men together in every aspect of church life will help us move towards a fuller vision of who we are: 'together, and individually, made in the image of God the Trinity: creator, mother, lover, friend, protector, sacrifice, redeemer, father, holy wisdom, mighty wind, vulnerable one, whispered word and blazing fire of love.'[20]

Above all, God is a God of relationship and it is to that aspect of our busy lives we now turn.

20. B. Baisley, 'Being realistic about feminism', in H. Wakeman (ed.), *Women Priests: The first years* (Darton, Longman and Todd, 1996), p. 109.

Friendship on the go

6

The yearning for meaningful relationships is something deep and instinctive. It is a basic human need, reflected in God's words after he had created the first human being – 'It is not good that the man should be alone'.

God has been communicating himself through relationships since the beginning of time. Our significant relationships are one of the primary ways in which God reaches us, through friends praying with us, children showing us what God is like, partners loving us. As someone once said, 'I know God loves me, but it sure feels good when someone with skin on shows me.'

Busyness as a cause of stress in relationships

There is no doubt that being *too* busy can affect the quality of our closest relationships, both the ability to form them in the first place and the capacity to maintain and cherish them. Many people just don't have the time it takes to make meaningful relationships. Where a long, slow engagement before marriage used to be the norm, now would-be couples take part in 'speed dating', in order to find out who they have an affinity with in the shortest time possible.

When relationships do form, the effects of busyness are more marked than ever. When I am most stressed about being too busy, the first people who feel the effects of my anxiety are my husband and children. I also know that when I am busy and enjoying it, when I am feeling fulfilled in doing all that is before me, they get a happier and more contented wife and mother.

Sometimes, though, the relationships themselves are the cause of the busyness and the stress. Sometimes the need to sustain and improve our closest relationships feels like a contribution to the busyness. We want to be the best parents we can be, the best lovers, the best friends, but all this takes time and energy. The sheer hard work involved in maintaining meaningful friendships can be overwhelming at times.

Our relationships have the capacity to be the anchors in our busy lives, rather than just another part of the stress, but we need to invest time in them to see them thrive and grow. We need to work out what are the priorities in our relating with people around us, and what could we let go of.

This chapter begins this exploration by looking at the gift of friendship as an important part of 'life in all its fullness'.

Messages

In a world where committed relationships, certainly marriage, are becoming less the norm, there is an increased emphasis on what friends can be for you. In many senses, friendship is the highest marker of what you can be for another person – 'She's not just my mother, she's my best friend', you will hear people saying. As family units are more dispersed and people move away from their places of birth and upbringing, the new network of relationships – friendships – take on added significance.

In a recent survey assessing 'social capital' (broadly defined as 'neighbourliness, social networks and civic participation') two-thirds of respondents said they had a 'satisfactory friendship net-work'. That is, they saw or spoke to friends at least once a week and had a close friend living nearby. Just over half had a 'satis-factory relatives network'. Twenty per cent had neither.[1]

It is not easy to find the time nor the space to make friendships:

Changing employment and education patterns, shifts in the use

1. General Household Survey, 2000, commissioned by the Health Development Agency, Office for National Statistics, www.statistics.gov.uk.

of leisure time (in particular around the viewing of television and other home-based forms of entertainment), the development of telephone and internet use, the more general move to the 'suburbs' and the rise of the nuclear family have had a major impact on the extent to which people engage in face-to-face relationships and belong to groups and associations.[2]

People today are yearning for close relationships, but are also growing increasingly wary of the commitment they might demand. There are an estimated 12 million bloggers, who use cyberspace to talk about their personal lives. One survey found that 52 per cent of them said the reason they posted their blogs was to share their personal experiences, to share with other anonymous people the subjects that matter in their personal lives. The Internet has created whole communities of friendly strangers.

Where does all this leave our notion of intimacy, when intimacy has always been based on the presumption that at some point at least you will physically be with the other person, in the flesh, as it were? One writer (of an article I read on the Internet, ironically) commented: 'Intimacy is based on the experience of being known and accepted as we truly are. Without actually being with another person, seeing and being seen, "flesh-to-flesh", true intimacy is by nature limited. It takes time to absorb another person's sharing of soul, time we may be reluctant to give.'[3]

What makes you happy? A survey done by the BBC to accompany a programme on happiness revealed that almost half of people – 48 per cent – say that having a close network of supportive relationships was the biggest factor in their happiness. Increased income only makes you happy up to a certain level. Above that, a committed network of supportive relationships is the thing that makes for a contented life. The converse is also true. A major factor leading to mental breakdown is a lack of significant relationships and supportive networks.

So we need friendships to be happy. But the thing about

2. M.E. Doyle and M.K. Smith, 'Friendship: Theory and experience', in *The Encyclopaedia of Informal Education* (2005).
3. Blair and Rita Justice in the *HealthLeader* online wellness magazine from the University of Texas Health Science Center, www.healthleader.uthouston.edu.

friendship is that it needs communication, effort, energy, care, love and time to survive. Friendship is time-consuming, which is fine if you only have one. Since Mat and I got married 14 years ago we have moved to a new area five times. We have lived in seven different neighbourhoods and belonged to four different church communities. In each of those places we have made new friends. We now have friends from university, friends we shared houses with, friends who are godparents to our children and we to theirs, friends we did our theological training with, friends we went on holiday with, friends who babysat for us, friends who supported us in our curacy, friends who were colleagues, friends we've met at the school gate, friends we lived in community with, friends we've worked with, friends we want to stay in touch with for ever, friends we're secretly quite relieved we've lost touch with, friends we just about manage Christmas-card exchange with, friends we will be with all our lives and new friends we are making at the moment. We even have friends we've made through other friends. I'm not saying this so that you'll think what lovely people we must be to have so many friends. I'm saying it because I think there are many people like us who have many friends, simply because they've lived in many different places and moved in many different circles. These are people who value their friendships very highly but who struggle to keep up with them all, to have the *time* to devote to them all.

I had a card the other day from a couple who we consider to be *the* best friends we have. It said this: 'We are so sorry for once again identifying ourselves as the most useless friends in your address book. Basically, my computer crashing (with your new address on it), a change of mobile phone, a staff away day and a church weekend stood between us and getting in touch with you.' We haven't been much better at being in touch with them. When friendships are so highly valued and are obviously such an important factor in our potential happiness, why is it so hard to find the time to invest in them?

A godly perspective

'Do not go to the house of your kindred in the day of your calamity. Better is a neighbour who is nearby than kindred who are far away' (Prov. 27.10). The writer seems to be saying that each of us needs to work at maintaining friendships, because when trouble comes, our close-at-hand friends will be more practically helpful than far-flung family. Family are important, of course, but this passage suggests that friends are sometimes of more practical use.

This does not exclude the fact that extended family can also be friends. The largest single source of help to us in our busy lives has been my mum and stepdad. They have looked after the children when we have needed them to. They have supported us financially. They have been there for us in every way possible. But then I consider them as friends as well as family.

Friendship is a very practical gift that we can offer to people who, for whatever reason, do not have the close support of their family – the bereaved, the divorced, those living in a country that is not their own. Friendships which are reliable are also important for cultivating local solidarity. In an age where people are often untrusting of each other and where society suffers as a result, friendship is very important. It is something that can be modelled by Christians as a way of challenging the individualism and ghetto mentality of contemporary culture. Our culture says, 'I will make friends only with people who are similar to me.' Christian friendship models something different. It can exist across boundaries of gender, culture and age as a sign of something new; a kingdom way of living.

Jesus and friendships

Jesus had great friends. He talked about friendship a lot. It is the word he used to describe his relationship with his followers: 'You are my friends if you do what I command you. I do not call you servants any longer, because the servant does not know what the master is doing; but I have called you friends, because I have made known to you everything that I heard from my father' (Jn 15.14–15).

I love the way Jesus related to his friends. Seeing the ways in which he cared for, laughed with, comforted and challenged them shows me a very real person to relate to. When I read of him affirming Martha in her recognition of who he is, I can believe that he would also affirm me in that way. When I hear him confronting Peter when he gets it so terribly wrong, and yet loving him anyway, I am encouraged that he would do the same for me. When I see him rebuking the men who criticized Mary as she anointed his feet in that lavish display of love and affection, I can imagine him standing up for me too. Jesus never married and did not have children, and so I can't imagine how he would have related in that way, but when I see him relating to his friends, it encourages me that he knows the joys and pains and reality of human relationships.

Jesus had deep and genuine friendships with both men and women. In a male-dominated society where the testimony of a woman was not recognized and women were seen as possessions along with sheep and donkeys, Jesus encourages and affirms women, not in a patronizing way, but as equals – as friends.

Arguably one of the closest friendships he had, alongside that of John and Peter, was his friendship with Mary of Magdala. My favourite passage in the Gospels is that spine-chillingly exciting encounter between Jesus and the grief-stricken Mary after his Resurrection, when he utters her name, 'Mary', and she sees him for who he is – not a gardener, but her greatest friend and her Lord. Jesus's intimate and vigorous relationship with Mary has been the source of much debate and controversy. Dan Brown's best-seller *The Da Vinci Code* suggested that Mary and Jesus were lovers, husband and wife and parents of a daughter. Speculation about the exact nature of the friendship between Jesus and Mary has been rife for many centuries. My feeling is it doesn't really matter exactly what type of relationship they had. If it was intimate, which it evidently was, the important thing is that Jesus models a closeness of relationship that shows he is able to identify with us in our close relationships, whether platonic or sexual.

One of the things we are often told is that friendship between men and women who are not romantically linked is not possible. In the film *When Harry Met Sally*, the two eponymous characters set out to be 'just good friends' and fail as the friendship turns into a sexual relationship. Jesus shows us something different, that friendship is good and is to be honoured and celebrated whether with members of the same sex as ourselves, or the other one.

Partnership and sacrifice

For Jesus, friendship was a high calling, but a costly one. He said, 'No one has greater love than this, to lay down one's life for one's friends' (Jn 15.13), which is exactly what he did. He knew all too well the painful wounds of his friendship with humanity. Friendship is costly. It involves sacrifice.

One of the major sacrifices it will involve is the sacrifice of time. In a busy life, where time is at a premium, it is very easy to allow friendships to be the thing that get knocked first off the To Do List. We *have* to go to work, we *have* to eat and our family obviously take immediate precedence, so time for friendship is often the first casualty in a time-pressured existence.

I know this very well. This evening, I have so much I could do, while the kids are in bed. I have a big pile of ironing, I have a list of jobs that need doing around the house, I could do some more writing of this book. But I also have a friend who phoned this morning and left a message on my answerphone saying she's having a hard time at the moment. Two friends wrote to me last week (one of them writing her phone number quite pointedly at the bottom of the letter), and I haven't got back to them yet. So I know the right thing to do is for me to spend the evening on the phone catching up with these three friends. But it's a sacrifice. Something else will have to go.

Friendships can be costly in another way too. To enter into a friendship with someone is to risk getting hurt by them. A line from Alfred, Lord Tennyson's poem *In Memoriam* says, 'Tis better to have loved and lost than never to have loved at all'. There is a risk attached to that loving. I saw many people in my role as chaplain at Lee Abbey who were nervous of committing to new friendships, because of residual fears left from former relationships that had gone wrong. When you've been rejected, or hurt, or sometimes even abused, it is very difficult to find the inner strength to love again, and this goes for friendship as much as for any relationship. Jesus must have known this. He knew that to invite us to be friends with him would involve a great sacrifice. It would involve him giving his life on the Cross. It would also involve the risk of rejection. And rejected he would be, and has been, over the centuries by millions of people with whom he would love to be friends, but who turn away.

Stepping above

If you are a busy person, it is all the more important to have friends and companions who give you energy, who fire you, who encourage you in your vocation, who inspire you, who release you from the pressures of life. Friendship offers the busy person many benefits.

Friends choose you

There is a well-known saying: 'You can choose your friends, but you can't choose your family.' Friendship is a matter of choice. You meet someone new, someone you work with, someone you live next door to, someone you go to church with. There might be many reasons to maintain an ongoing relationship of sorts with that person: politeness, convenience, obligation, loyalty. But friendship will only develop with people you *choose* to be friends with – because you like them, because you share interests, because something between you just 'clicks', because there's a chemistry between you. If someone chooses to have you as their friend, it's very affirming. It helps you to feel valued for who you are. Some friends will value you for what you do, but not the best ones.

Genuine friendships are therefore a good antidote to busyness. When you are valued not for what you do but for who you are, the perceived pressure to 'do more' is relieved. I have friends who enjoy the fact that I am a clergyperson. Perhaps they are too and it means we can share tales of joy and woe (and funerals); perhaps it is because they have benefited in some way from my ministry. Maybe they like my preaching, maybe I took their wedding or baptized their baby. My best friends know that being ordained is only part of who I am and it isn't a central feature of our friendship. I have friends whom I know I could tell I had decided to become a road sweeper, and that would be OK by them. I would hope they might question the wisdom of my planned career change, but they'd still be there for me.

Friendship is great for busy people because the true friend says, 'Yes I love what you do, I'm impressed by the way you live your life or do your job, but you matter to me, not what you do'.

Friends help you to know you are not alone

C.S. Lewis said:

> Friendship arises out of mere Companionship when two or more of the companions discover that they have in common some insight or interest or even taste which the others do not share and which, till that moment, each believed to be his own unique treasure (or burden). The typical expression of opening Friendship would be something like, 'What? You too? I thought I was the only one'.[4]

The best friends I have are those who share with me some aspect of my life – a shared time at university, a shared interest, a shared love of shopping and so on. There is no greater friend than the one to

4. C.S. Lewis, *The Four Loves* (HarperCollins, 2002), pp. 78–9.

whom you can say, 'I feel like this about that', and they reply 'Do you really? So do I!'

I remember this aspect of friendship being a real comfort when my children were very young. When you're going through it, there's a tendency to feel that you're the only one who has a baby who doesn't sleep, doesn't eat and cries all the time. The test of a true friendship comes with potty training. When our son was struggling to master the art of pooing anywhere other than in his pants, we thought we were the only ones struggling with this aspect of child development. We went to visit some friends of ours who had a similar-aged child. Our friendship was well and truly forged in steel when they admitted that their daughter pooed in her pants as well. It's amazing what solidarity emerges with an admission of a shared struggle.

Friends help you to see yourself honestly

'Better is open rebuke than hidden love. Well meant are the wounds a friend inflicts, but profuse are the kisses of an enemy' (Prov. 27.5–6). True friendship isn't about being slushy. True friendship does not exist to tell you you're wonderful all the time. True friendship offers love which might sometimes be painful, finding the right balance between encouragement and challenge; the reassuring and the bracing. There are always things about ourselves we don't want to know but it is up to our friends to 'wound' us – and make us healthier people. When the sparks fly in a friendship, the result can be a sharpening that is healthy. Prov. 27.17 says 'Iron sharpens iron, and one person sharpens the wits of another.' The Hebrew here actually translates, 'One person sharpens the *face* of another'. That is what real friendship is about, facing up to the healthy clash of personalities and views and growing as a result. As we continually make contact with our friends, something changes in us; we are moulded and shaped by them. Contemporary culture says: 'Avoid conflict at all costs. Being nice to each other is what matters – even if it means being two-faced. Gossip is OK. Good, honest confrontation is not.' A Christian model of friendship is different. Friends sharpen each other, speaking the truth in love, as Ephesians ch. 4 puts it: 'Be angry, but do not sin; do not let the sun go down on your anger.'

One of the ways in which we might invite our friends to 'sharpen' us in this way is by asking their opinion on our busyness. Whether or not we are making wise choices about what we do with our time might be easier for our friends to discern for us than for us to discern in ourselves. So get together with your friends, open a bottle of wine and ask them what they think about your busyness.

Friends aren't afraid of speaking the truth

When new members join the Lee Abbey community, they are asked to make a set of promises about their faith in Christ and about the vision and values of community living. One of them goes like this: 'Are you prepared to learn to live in fellowship, being open to be known for who you are, accepting one another in love, and saying of others nothing that could not be said to them personally if love and wisdom required it?' If you were to ask any community member which promise they found the hardest to keep, they would say this one. Saying nothing of each other behind their backs has a flip side – being prepared to say difficult things to their face if that was necessary.

Conflict is one of the hardest things to get right in any relationship. In a community, it is essential that conflict is 'done well', to enable it to be a valuable tool of God's grace and forgiveness and growth. However, learning to speak honestly and wisely to one's friends is one of the hardest lessons. Niceness is the great enemy of good relationships because it means that we fail to address deeper problems in favour of sweeping them under the carpet.

I'm rubbish at conflict. I prefer everything to remain 'nice'. Living in community at Lee Abbey, I did learn that conflict is inevitable, especially when you live and work so closely to others. I learned the *theory* that it is better to be honest with one's friends and sort things out, rather than stewing in your juices, but I'm still not very good at it.

Friends take the focus away from yourself

Problems, issues and concerns can seem very large when dealt with on your own. It is very easy when very busy to become self-absorbed, obsessed even, with yourself and what you are doing. Some of my best friends are those who can help me to get a little perspective on life, to laugh at myself and not take myself quite so seriously.

David Runcorn (a friend of mine, actually) points to the particular importance of this function in friendships for clergy: 'For me one of the greatest gifts of friendship is that I can stop being responsible! We need helping taking time off being God. It is not good for us anyway.'[5]

Soul friendship

There is a great benefit in having some friends who are wise, trustworthy and who know you well whom you can turn to when things get tough, or when you have a major decision to make. I have appreciated wholeheartedly the value of such friendships. There are two or three of my friends whom I know I can talk things through with and pray with.

Increasingly this kind of friendship is taking on an intentional and deliberate form and being called various things like 'spiritual direction' or 'mentoring' or 'soul friendship'. A soul friend or spiritual director is someone with whom you meet at regular intervals to discuss your life, your faith and the direction both are taking. The function of a soul friend 'is to help the seeker discover where they are, and what should be their next steps in their journey through life, in the light of eternity'.[6]

The need for this kind of wise friendship is all the more important when you take into account our busy lifestyles. As Ray

5. David Runcorn, 'Self-management', in *The Vicar's Guide* (Church House Publishing, 2005), p. 36.
6. Ray Simpson, *Soul Friendship: Celtic insights into spiritual mentoring* (Hodder and Stoughton, 1999), p. 14.

Simpson points out: 'The massive increase in technology, data, mobility and choice means that we have more opportunities available to us than ever before. We have to make more and quicker decisions. We can easily make bad decision through lack of a wise friend with whom we can talk things through.'[7]

Although people might say that they don't have time for this kind of regular meeting with a soul friend, when put in these terms, you might not be able to afford not to.

7. Ibid., p. 12.

For better and for worse

My kids are fond of asking me, 'Mummy, were you alive in the olden days?' (My son even asked me the other day whether I was around before wheels were invented.) In a way, marriage looked a lot easier in 'the olden days', when husbands went out to work and wives stayed at home in spotty aprons and washed the dishes. I may be wrong, but it strikes me that probably not a lot of negotiation went on in the olden days about gender roles and whose turn it was to put out the rubbish and whose turn it was to work that day. There are some on the evangelical right who would love us to return to the olden days. There the answer lies, they say. If women just stopped trying to be like men and men acted more like, well, men, then everything would be all right. Women at home, men at work. Sorted.

I'm glad I wasn't alive in the olden days. I would not have been able to pursue my calling to be a priest. I would have gone mad making all that jam, and I would have missed out on the chance to share together all that life holds for both of us, husband and wife, mummy and daddy, man and woman, Revd Ineson and Revd Ineson, Mat and Emma.

Messages

But first, a very brief look at the changing pattern of marriage in the UK today. For a start, fewer people are getting married at all. There were 311,180 weddings in the UK in 2004. For the past three years the number of people getting married has increased very slightly. However, there has been a previous long-term decline from the peak number of 480,285 marriages in 1972.

People are also getting married later. The average age of women at first marriage was 22.6 in 1971, 28.9 years in 2003.[1]

The rate of marriage breakdown is at the highest it has ever been, although the rate of divorce has actually fallen since 2001, especially in younger couples. The amount of sex married couples have has declined since the 1950s (of course this decline in quantity may well correspond with a rise in quality, but I don't know how they'd test that!). Researchers from the Kinsey Institute found that 42 per cent of women who cohabit with male partners have sex two or three times a week. This compares with 33 per cent of married women. Dr John Bancroft, the Institute's director, said:

> People don't have as much sex as they used to. Couples are often weighted down by double careers and childcare, and by the time people have been to the shopping mall and watched all the television they want, there is not much time for sex. . . . We live in an age where there is little unfilled leisure time. Sex used to fill that gap.[2]

We live in an age where we are busier than ever. How do you 'busy-proof' your marriage, whatever roles you both take? In some senses, the knocking down of the traditional bastions of male and female roles has made things more complicated and busier. But my generation has been brought up to believe, and our experience has shown us, that equality is possible in all areas of life, that marriage is about a partnership of equals. What people do with their lives is more about what they have the gifts and abilities to do than what their biological sex prescribes they ought to do. I believe the Bible offers this kind of vision of what marriage can be too.

A godly perspective

From the beginning, from that first joyful expression of similarity, equality and mutuality that Adam uttered when he saw Eve –

1. Mintel market research, www.mintel.com.
2. 'No sex please, we're too busy', article on www.bbc.co.uk.

'bone of my bone, flesh of my flesh!' – marriage was intended to be a partnership. Man and woman together are blessed by God for the task of caring for this world and for each other: 'Therefore a man leaves his father and his mother and clings to his wife, and they become one flesh' (Gen. 2.24).

One of the most painful effects of the sin that entered the world at the Fall was the severing of the love, trust and equality of this one-flesh bond. One of the effects of their disobedience is that they are doomed to fulfil less than equal roles in life. The woman will allow herself to be dominated and the man will take power over her: 'To the woman he said, "I will greatly increase your pangs in childbearing; in pain you shall bring forth children, yet your desire shall be for your husband, and he shall rule over you"' (Gen. 3.16). Far from being God's best intention for men and women and their relating together, the effects of the Fall are devastating, unacceptable and should be worked against: 'Genesis 3:16–17 is best understood as a description of the new order of things, of how life *will* be lived as a result of the Fall, rather than how it *should* be lived ... The result of these judgements is loss of harmony in relationships.'[3]

The reason Christ died on the Cross was to redeem *all* fallen relationships, between God and humankind, between fellow human beings, between the earth and its inhabitants and between men and women. Christians are therefore to work with God towards the full reconciliation of all these relationships, including in the relating of men and women, and especially in marriage.

One of the 'benefits of his passion', signed and sealed by the coming at Pentecost of the redeeming Holy Spirit of Jesus, is the breaking down of traditional barriers that have existed since the Fall:

> In the last days it will be, God declares, that I will pour out my Spirit upon all flesh, and your sons and your daughters shall prophesy, and your young men shall see visions, and your old

---

3. Richard S. Hess, 'Equality with and without innocence' in Ronald W. Pierce and Rebecca Merrill Groothuis (eds), *Discovering Biblical Equality: Complementary without hierarchy* (IVP, 2004), p. 92.

men shall dream dreams. Even upon my slaves, both men and women, in those days I will pour out my Spirit; and they shall prophesy. (Peter quoting Joel 2.28–32 in Acts 2.17–18)

Paul is very clear that one of the effects of being 'in Christ' is that the old order of things has gone and a new order has come: 'So if anyone is in Christ, there is a new creation: everything old has passed away; see, everything has become new!' (2 Cor. 5.17). This 'new creation' for men and women heralds equality in all areas of life:

In Christ Jesus you are all children of God through faith. As many of you as were baptized into Christ have clothed your-selves with Christ. There is no longer Jew or Greek, there is no longer slave or free, there is no longer male and female; for all of you are one in Christ Jesus. And if you belong to Christ, then you are Abraham's offspring, heirs according to the promise. (Gal. 3.26–29)

Equality is restored in previously fractured relationships in the context of being the body of Christ. But each man and woman is to continue to play their part in bringing in the reality of God's new order on earth, an 'expression of the new order and new humanity that is already present, even while it is yet to be'.[4]

On the surface of it, the Bible is not necessarily the best place to find validation for good relating between men and women. The Old Testament is full of polygamy (Solomon had 700 wives and numerous concubines), incest (a Jewish man would be required to marry any widow to whom he was the closest living relative) and abuse (the rape of Tamar in 2 Sam. 13 is a particularly disturbing example).

Jesus himself seemed to be singularly (pardon the pun) uncon-cerned with marriage and family relationships in comparison with the important task of bringing in God's kingdom on earth (see, for example, Mt. 12.46–50 and Mt 19.29), although his teaching on

4. Gordon D. Fee, 'Male and Female in the New Creation', in Pierce and Groothuis (eds), *Discovering Biblical Equality*, p. 185.

divorce does signal the high regard in which he held justice and fidelity in the marriage relationship. The bachelor Paul had a seemingly indifferent view of marriage, writing that celibacy is a preferred choice for the unmarried Christian (1 Cor. 7.1–2 and 7:7–9).

However, marriage is the metaphor used to speak of God's love for his people (in particularly poignant imagery in the book of Hosea) and of Christ's relationship with the Church in the consummation that will come at the end of time: 'And I saw the holy city, the new Jerusalem, coming down out of heaven from God, prepared as a bride adorned for her husband' (Rev. 21.2).

Partnership and sacrifice

What is the secret of a happy marriage? An article in the *Guardian* printed an interview with Lucy and Harold Allgood, who have been happily married to each other for 78 years. Yes, 78. They were 22 when they were married and they're now both 101. What stands out most as they talked were the 'sacrifices and compromises they have subsequently made – and the particular joys they have brought each other'.[5] Both sacrifice and joy are keys to a successful marriage.

Sometimes people ask me how I manage to do so many things. There is one answer really – because I have a husband who supports everything I do. And I support him. Our marriage is not perfect, far from it. But we have discovered that in order to live life in all its fullness we've got to be in it together. Our marriage must be one of absolute equality in the way identified by Sue Walrond-Skinner:

> The essential characteristics that differentiate the equal partner marriage is that everything is negotiable except the principle that everything is negotiable; decision-making is shared on the basis of achieving justice and care for both, and each partner is

5. Yvonne Roberts, 'Lucy and Harold', *Guardian*, 11 November 2006.

enabled to function effectively in the spheres of paid work outside the home and family work inside it.[6]

In more 'theological' language it is about mutual sacrifice, mutual respect, mutual submission, mutual support – and a very good sense of humour.

The key concept for us is mutuality, defined as 'the bi-directional movement of feelings, thoughts and activity between persons in relationships'[7] and much more poetically expressed as 'the two will become one flesh'. Paul puts it another way in 1 Cor. 7.4; 'the wife does not have authority over her own body, but the husband does; likewise the husband does not have authority over his own body, but the wife does.' A belongs to B in the same way that B belongs to A. There is equality and mutuality, love and respect in this kind of arrangement. But how is it worked out in practice, and how does it help us in our busyness?

Mutual submission

Despite his wonderful description of the 'new order' outlined above, what Paul says about marriage elsewhere in his letters seems to go against his obvious promotion of equality in the body of Christ. However, we have to see what he said about many things, including marriage, in the context of his total obsession with spreading the gospel before the imminent return of Christ. Anything that gets in the way of this is to be pushed aside.

Paul therefore encourages believers to continue to be respectful of prevailing cultural norms, 'where the husband, father and master are the same person – the patron (hopefully benevolent) of his wife, children and slaves'.[8] For the sake of the spread of the gospel, wives

---

6. Sue Walrond-Skinner, *Double Blessing* (Mowbray 1998), p. 64.
7. N.P. Genero, J.B. Miller, J. Surrey and L.M. Baldwin, 'Measuring perceived mutuality in close relationships: Validation of the mutual psychological development questionnaire', in *Journal of Family Psychology* (1992), 6, pp. 36–48, quoted in Walrond-Skinner, *Double Blessing*, p. 66.
8. Fee, 'Male and Female in the New Creation', in Pierce and Groothuis (eds), *Discovering Biblical Equality*, p. 183.

are to continue to submit to the authority of their husbands according to the cultural norms of the day, as slaves are to submit to their masters. The conventions of the time presupposed that 'an insubordinate wife was a bad witness for the gospel in a situation where non-Christian husbands expected subordination'.[9] So in Col. 3.18–19, the wife is called upon to submit to her husband.

These were early days for the Church living in the new order of Christ, and any cultural changes that were too sudden or extreme might have hindered the spread of the gospel and the good standing of Christians in the community. Paul wanted neither of these things to happen, so he suggests that wives continue in the submissive roles. Husbands, however, are given new commands to love their wives – something that has not been said in the culture before. There is change, but it is gradual.

Now 2,000 years later, we have come a long way. In today's cultural climate, to continue to teach and preach wifely submission could be said to hinder the spread of the gospel in a world where women are in positions of authority in all aspects of life and work. In Eph. 5.18, Paul encourages believers to 'submit to one another out of reverence for Christ' (NIV). In so doing both husband and wife love, both husband and wife submit and both husband and wife discover the freedom of God's calling upon their lives. That seems to me to be a different, prophetic way of living today.

I didn't promise to obey Mat when we married, as we both knew there was no point in my making a promise that neither of us would want me to keep, nor that I would have been able to promise in all conscience. The symmetry of our marriage vows to each other expressed very clearly the mutual partnership that our marriage would become. The theology of mutual submission has been a keystone of our marriage. It is possible. It does work and you don't have to tie yourself in convoluted knots to do it.

A few words about what mutual submission is not. It's not about trying to outdo each other in submission, playing a kind of 'how low can you go' game. Mat plays this stupid game with our dog where he tries to get his head lower than hers. If you know

9. I. Howard Marshall, 'Mutual love and submission in marriage', in Pierce and Groothuis (eds), *Discovering Biblical Equality*, p. 192.

anything about dogs you'll know that they see themselves as members of a pack, and that to submit to the authority of the pack leader you must always hold your head lower than theirs. You sometimes see dogs 'play bowing' when they meet new dogs in the park. Our dog considers Mat the pack leader in our house (no, I'm not going to go into the theology of that – he simply feeds her more often). So Mat winds the dog up by trying to get his head lower than hers. They end up in this ridiculous position with them both lying face down on the floor. Mutual submission in marriage is not like that! In fact it's more about building the other person up than putting yourself down. It is not about being a doormat for the other person to walk on. It is not about simply putting up with unreasonable or disrespectful or oppressive behaviour just because you're submitting. In any case, if submission is mutual there would never be any need for this.

Mutual submission is not about continually submitting absolutely equally at every moment, or playing a kind of 'I've submitted, now it's your turn' game. At times, one may lay down more of their lives than the other out of the practical necessity of life circumstances. You may need to submit to each other's godly callings at different times in your lives. We have friends who try to take it in turns whose job demands when and where they move. Their last move was led by her job, the one before that by his. They don't do this because it's 'fair' but because it's a sensible, practical and loving way for them to make family decisions.

Living a life and a marriage of mutual submission simply means that you get to know each other really well and therefore you are aware of each other's needs and are prepared to consider them above your own: 'Trust is the core reward that develops when spouses regard each other with mutual respect that puts priority on the relationship, when each spouse treats the other as a cherished equal, one who is uniquely gifted as God's creation.'[10]

10. Judith K. Balswick and Jack O. Balswick, 'Marriage as a partnership of Equals', in Pierce and Groothuis (eds), *Discovering Biblical Equality*, p. 458.

Mutual sacrifice

Some partnerships cite the 'servant leadership' model of male headship, which holds that the man is to love his wife like Christ, who laid down his life for the Church. What can happen all too often in practice, though, is that the husband loves his wife, certainly, but that she lays down her preferences, desires and needs again and again at his feet.

A truer model is one where *both* partners make sacrifices for the other. That may at times be an unequal sacrifice, the sacrifice of one for the sake of the other, for instance in the case of one of the partners being struck down by illness. But the assumption is that sacrifice from both husband and wife, for the good of the other and the marriage, is *equally* possible: 'making the best interest of the other a priority is the essence of the extraordinary way of the cross and covenant love'.[11] That's what mutual sacrifice means. Not that you both lay down your life for the other constantly and equally. Again, that would end up in an impossible competition to see who can lay down the most. It does mean that both husband and wife, man and woman, are equally able and willing to sacrifice something for the sake of the other, after talking and making decisions together.

This kind of sacrifice is very real to me at the moment. As with our recent move, I have chosen not to do a job, or a specific role in ministry. I've been writing this book, and I do a small amount of pastoral work, but I have 'sacrificed' the right to a full-time expression of my own ministry at this time. Making that transition has been quite hard. For many years my identity has been bound up in being a priest, and in being a pioneering one at that. Laying down the right to any official role in the Church or at work has been quite tough. But then, no choices in life are without cost and sacrifice. If we choose to be busy, but not over-busy, and to have healthy marriages to boot, then it is likely that something will have to go. Jesus knows all about sacrifice. And he honours sacrifices made for others, especially our families.

Sacrifice in marriage relationships is a radical concept in today's culture. Marriage today often seems to be sustained only for as long

11. Ibid., p. 449.

as it is good for you. Prenuptial agreements are based on the fact that the marriage is conditional as long as it continues to offer discernible benefits for the individual – 'I will love you as long as it works for me (and afterwards I want my share of the money)'. Christian marriage needs to model something different, based on a God whose covenant love is entirely unconditional. The whole Christian message proclaims the shocking value of doing things for others even when you don't get the benefit (turning the other cheek, going the extra mile and so on). It is based on the ethos of laying down one's life for the good of another, following the example of Jesus, who didn't go to the Cross saying, 'So, what's in it for me?'

Mutual support

Mutual support and empowerment is 'a reciprocal process of building up, equipping, supporting, encouraging, affirming and challenging the other'.[12]

Both of you deserve this kind of support. I worry about wives of church leaders who tell me that their primary vocation in life is to support their husband in his ministry. I want to ask them, 'And is his primary vocation in life to support you in yours?' Whatever you believe about different roles for men and women, inequality of support is something to be wary of in marriage. I know someone who is afraid of asking her husband to do anything twice for fear of being seen as nagging. That kind of fear comes not out of mutuality and respect but out of a wrong sense of the role and purpose of marriage for both partners.

I realized some time ago that every time Mat did a housework job around the house, I thanked him for doing it. It was a habit I'd got into. But what it suggested to both of us was that when Mat did his share of the housework, I saw it as his 'doing me a favour'. So now I don't thank him and he doesn't need to thank me, because housework is our shared, mutual responsibility, not something he does 'to help me out'. We support each other

12. Ibid., p. 460.

equally and one of the ways in which we do this is to share the housework.

There are deeper, more significant ways in which couples must support each other, obviously. When life gets tough, in unemployment, illness, bereavement, depression, the need to support becomes all the more real. It is at times like these that the foundations laid by having a mutual marriage will bear fruit. If your practice has been to support each other, when there is the need for particular support of one of the partners, the other is more likely to have the self-assurance and the strength to respond. What happens when both of you are going though a hard time is the subject of the next chapter.

Mutual admiration

People often ask whether Mat and I are competitive: 'Do you compare notes on who preaches the best sermons?' The answer is that the concept of being competitive means very little, because we both want the other to succeed so much, that it doesn't matter if the other person is 'better' or 'worse' at something. What matters is that they are fulfilling their own potential.

If marriage is to be a true marriage of equals you have to see it as your life's mission to help your spouse to succeed. You *both* have to want to support each other, to see *each other* fulfilled and happy, balanced, successful, at peace – whatever is good in life. It's a philosophy encapsulated in Paul's words: 'Do nothing from selfish ambition or conceit, but in humility regard others as better than yourselves. Let each of you look not to your own interests, but to the interests of others' (Phil. 2.3–4).

There is a longstanding popular tradition, found especially in comedy sketches about marriage, of putting one's husband or wife down: 'My husband is hopeless at . . .' It may be funny on the TV but it's not very good in real life for nurturing a feeling of mutual admiration and support.

In a mutual marriage, it's all a lot easier if you think your spouse is just about the best thing that ever walked the earth. Let's not get too sloppy and 'Mills and Boon' about it. You don't ignore their faults. But there has to be a genuine and mutual admiration for the gifts, qualities and personality of your partner. You have to think they're amazing. It's summed up by Virginia Woolf: 'My heart stood still with pride that he had ever married me.'[13] Don't put each other down, build each other up where at all possible, in public as well as in private.

Stepping above

So how does all this mutuality and equality help with busyness? In some ways, it doesn't. Living a mutual lifestyle throws up challenges of communication, negotiation and juggling that probably aren't experienced in traditional marriages where roles are more clearly defined. However, there are huge and unmissable benefits to mutuality.

Firstly, equality and mutuality have been associated with 'successful' marriage.[14] If you live a busy and stressful life, it is simply stating the obvious that a successful marriage or partnership will alleviate your stress and support you in your endeavours. Conversely an unsuccessful marriage will exacerbate stress.

Secondly, if you see yourselves as equals, you work things out together. You see the marriage unit as a whole. You make life choices as a whole. And you deal with busyness and stress as a whole, asking, 'What can we do for each other?' as well as 'What are my needs?'

Thirdly, research has shown that couples who experience mutuality in their married life have an increased sense of vitality and ability to take action, flowing from an increased sense of self-worth and validation.[15] Being able to do and achieve more, and an

13. Woolf, quoted in Roberts, 'Lucy and Harold', *Guardian*.
14. See, e.g., Claire Low Rabin, *Equal partners, Good friends: Empowering couples through therapy* (Routledge, 1996).
15. Genero *et al.*, 'Measuring perceived mutuality in close relationships', pp. 36–48, quoted in Walrond-Skinner, *Double Blessing*, p. 66.

increased sense of energy and confidence, are beneficial in the fight against feeling over-busy.

Every couple is different and lives in the midst of different circumstances. Take some time to talk about what mutuality in the way described in this chapter might mean *for you*. Ask some questions of the way you've always done things. And if you need to make some changes, be courageous and do so.

Busy-proof your marriage

It is possible for busy people today to maintain a healthy, happy, mutual marriage. I offer the following seven strategies for developing a mutual marriage in the fast lane.

Put your marriage first

There is (almost) nothing more important. If you are married, and a Christian, your primary vocation is to be a child of God and a disciple of Jesus Christ. Your second is to your spouse and family, and your third is to your area of work or ministry. Nothing should get in the way of the time and energy you need for your marriage relationship – not job, not church, not leisure, not even children. I once heard it said that the best thing a father can do for a child is to love the child's mother. And vice versa. Strengthen and protect your marriage relationship and you will be surprised how much of the rest of life falls into a rightful perspective.

Spend time together

Get over thinking it's wrong to put time with your spouse in your diary. If you are living a mutual marriage partnership, you'll have to have good diaries anyway, so schedule in time with your partner where you can relax and continue to get to know each other. The theologian Stanley Hauerwas once famously said that you always marry the wrong person. By this he meant that the person you married will not always be the person you married – they will change and develop – and so will you. That's why it is important to spend time together so you continue to know and appreciate this changing person.

Mat and I try to put in one evening a week where we do nothing very much together. It usually involves a bottle of wine, a curry and a DVD. We may not talk that much. But it's our time and it's precious. We also try and have a weekend every year where we go away together alone without the children. It's a time for us to spend some decent time together and remember why we married each other.

People talk about having quality time with your loved one. In my experience, it is not possible to have *quality* time until you also have a decent *quantity* of time. It's no use ignoring each other all month and then having a frantic half an hour of 'quality time' and expecting your relationship to be hunky-dory. You can't 'binge' on time spent together, starving yourself for months and then having a long session. That evening a week 'feeds' the weekend a year. Consistency is the key.

Do things you both enjoy

Find a hobby you both like. Some of my friends have discovered a passion for salsa dancing classes with their spouses. You can't tell me that something like that won't add a bit of va-va-voom to a marriage! It doesn't have to be expensive. Get a dog. Some of our best times talking and mulling things over happen as we walk the dog in the park. The action of spending time together doing something you both find relaxing and life-giving will enrich and enhance your marriage.

Accept lower standards in the things that don't matter

Accepting lower standards in less important matters enables you to put time into the things that do – namely your marriage. As with all the areas covered in this book, a choice to put more time into one thing will inevitably involve a certain degree of sacrifice in another. If you are really going to put your marriage first, something else might have to go. I don't advise that this something else is time with your children or family. But it may be that extra hour at the office or that other thing you do in church or that night out with the lads.

Accept slightly lower standards in the things that don't *really* matter. Housework is the obvious thing. I say this as someone who finds this hard! I like doing housework (see Chapter 7 on this) and I like the feeling it gives me of control and order. Mat will only notice our bedroom is messy if he can't actually find the bed under a pile of clothes. Part of the compromise for us has been his learning to clear things up before they drive me mental, and my learning that it doesn't actually matter all that much if things are a little bit messy sometimes.

Don't let the romance die

One of the biggest causes of lack of interest in sex is over-busyness and stress. If you work together and share every area of your life, that can be doubly true. Keeping the romance alive when you're equal in every way can be a tough call. At times Mat and I have admitted that at night sometimes it feels more like going to bed with a colleague rather than a lover (and it's generally accepted that you're not meant to do 'that kind of thing' with your colleagues!). We need constantly to remind ourselves not to neglect intimacy and to work at being loving in addition to being well organized and efficient. We have a rule that we *have to* kiss each other last thing before going to sleep, after we've turned off the light. It means we remember that the other person in bed with us is our lover and not our colleague. It also prevents us from 'letting the sun go down on your anger'. It's very difficult to kiss someone you're still mad with (although sometimes I have to admit the kiss can resemble a head-butt, but that's only if I'm *really* mad).

Keep communicating, even when you don't feel like it

The key to it all is communication. It is so important. Sometimes it takes an awful lot of hard work to communicate properly. It is tiring. Communicating well doesn't mean talking about everything that comes into your head. But it does mean not burying things that would be better aired. It does mean being honest with each other about your feelings, your needs and your fears. It does mean not assuming anything on the part of your partner and always checking things that matter with them.

Laugh a lot

I think the one thing that has kept our marriage strong in the midst of the chaos and busyness of shared ministry, marriage and parenting (apart from God, obviously) is a sense of humour. We laugh together a lot. Every day. We have a similar sense of humour and the same things make us laugh. Over the years we've built up a stock of shared funny moments and phrases that would probably make you cringe if I mentioned any of them to you, but which make us crease every time. If you're going to do this mutuality thing, you have to be able to place your marriage in the highest place of significance. You also have to learn not to take it, or your spouse, or yourself, too seriously.

You've got to laugh . . .

Busy with the kids

8

Some of the busiest people I know are parents with young children. Research carried out by the Home-Start charity to launch the 'Real Parents' campaign found that many parents of young children struggle: 'more than two thirds said their life was easier before having children, one in four admitted they didn't cope easily and nearly one in five worry that other people are more competent parents. When asked what they found most difficult about being a parent of under 5s, the overwhelming majority – more than a quarter – cited "lack of sleep", while one in ten said it was "not having enough time in the day".[1]

Children are messy, smelly, impolite, inconsiderate, selfish, energy-draining, time-consuming – and expensive. Latest estimates put the cost of raising a child at £180,000. That is an increase of 28 per cent in the last four years.[2]

The thing is, they're also a delightful, wonderful, precious gift of God. I don't say this lightly. For me, the most difficult, the most challenging and undoubtedly the most joyful aspect of the past 11 years has been being a mother to my two children. They are absolutely the most important thing in my life and I would cheerfully die for them at any point. The greatest, most treasured compliment anyone can give me is that I am a good mum.

When time is at a premium, it is easy to see children as a burden rather than a blessing and to simply 'get by' as a mother or father. And to feel incredibly guilty in the process.

The dilemma is this: do we shoe horn our children into our busyness, do we make them fit, or do we make choices that enable us to mould the rest of our lives around having them and raising them? Perhaps like me you are eager to do the best for your

1. www.realparents.org.uk.
2. Survey by Liverpool Victoria insurance providers.

children above all else, but wonder how to do that in the midst of a busy life. If so, leave your guilt here and read on.

Messages

Changing patterns of childbirth and parenting

Twenty years ago, the average woman had her first child at 25. Today the average for first-time mothers is 29. Two years ago, the number of babies born to women aged 30 to 34 overtook the number born to women aged 25 to 29. Around one in five women currently reaching the end of their fertile life is childless. This compares with one in ten women born in the mid-1940s.[3]

There are several reasons for this. More and more women today are choosing to work outside the home before they have children. There is a feeling that they want to get their career established before they take a break to have children. House prices also contribute to couples delaying having children 'until we can afford them'. One survey found that two-thirds of a sample of childless adults under the age of 45 said they were delaying having children until they could save enough to meet the expense incurred with raising a family. Half were postponing having a family until they could move to a bigger home.[4]

The fact that many women are delaying having children until later in life has implications both for the number of children they have and for the relative ease they find in getting pregnant. Rates of fertility in women drop dramatically after the age of 35 and more women are finding that delaying starting a family comes with a price. In an editorial in the *British Medical Journal*, fertility expert Dr Susan Bewley is quoted as saying: 'Women want to "have it all", but biology is unchanged. Deferring defies Nature and risks heartbreak. If women want room to manoeuvre, they are unwise

---

3. Office for National Statistics, www.statistics.gov.uk.
4. Cited by John Carvel, *Guardian*, 4 October 2006.

to wait till their 30s.'[5] The number of couples seeking help with conception through IVF has increased considerably. Women are being encouraged by some fertility experts to freeze their eggs while they are young 'if children are in their life plan, but the time is not yet right for them'. Increasing advances in fertility treatment do mean that it is possible for women to have children later in life, but is it always a good idea to wait?

Prevailing culture seems to see children as another commodity that we gain or another task to be achieved in our jam-packed lives. The increasingly widespread attitude that it is my 'right' to have children when it suits me, begs the question whether we have come to see children as just another part of our busy lives that we will 'fit in somewhere', or 'achieve' when it suits us. Some people talk as if children were something else you 'have' or 'own' or 'have a right to'. One woman on a television documentary about couples receiving genetic fertility treatment decided she wanted a daughter as well as the two sons she already had. Rather than taking 'pot luck' with the third child, she and her husband underwent complex genetic testing on embryos fertilized in the laboratory (abroad) in order to ensure their success at having a daughter. She said in that programme: 'To have a daughter before I die is a big ambition for me.' When a child is 'my right' and one of each is 'my ambition', what does that say about the way we view children and parenthood?

At the tender age of 22, Mat and I were contemplating whether to have our first child or not. I was in the middle of doing a PhD and I knew I wanted a career (at that time I thought it might be as a university lecturer). We didn't have much money, Mat was commuting a long distance to work as an engineer, and we wanted to travel in the future. In many ways it was not a convenient time to have a baby. But we both knew that if we did nothing else in life, we wanted to be parents. So we decided to 'try it and see what happens'. We figured it would probably take a while to get pregnant anyway. Wrong. We hit the jackpot first time (much to the disappointment of Mat who had been looking forward to practising a little more). I am so glad we had Molly when we did. It means we

5. Dr Susan Bewley, Dr Melanie Davies and Professor Peter Braude, 'Which Career First?', *British Medical Journal*, reported in *Times Online* (www.timesonline.co.uk), 16 September 2005.

will be young enough to enjoy her as she gets older and when one day she (hopefully) has children of her own we will be young enough to be lively and energetic grandparents! Having a child so young has not stopped us from achieving any of the ambitions we have had. We've both worked, we've travelled, we've lived life to the full, and all with Molly (and later her brother Toby) in tow. We haven't had much money, but – hey, money isn't everything.

Now I'm not saying: 'We got it right! Do it like us, everyone!' I know that circumstances are different for every couple. I know some people don't meet the love of their life until later on, I know some people have real and painful difficulty with conception, I know some people's life circumstances make it just about impossible to have children until later. But as a principle I wish more people would put the choice to have a baby above all else, while it's early enough to be an easy choice.

Doing it well

Before I had my daughter, I had been used to achieving in everything. I had organized my life and was in control of everything I did. I assumed I would be equally successful, organized and controlled as a mother. I would give birth naturally, I would breastfeed beautifully every four hours exactly, my child would sleep at night and cry only when wet or hungry. When she napped in the daytime I would write up my doctorate. Ha, ha. Those ideals started to evaporate about 12 hours into a 20-hour labour, shortly before the epidural and the emergency Caesarean section. Molly cried constantly for her first year and hardly slept. After about three months I was a fat, frazzled, exhausted wreck. It was a kindly midwife who pointed out to me that women who had previously been 'successful and in control' were invariably those who struggled most with babies, because babies can't be measured by success and they, not you, usually call the shots. Once I accepted that this was the way it was, and went with the flow a little more, things started to fall into place. I learned to relax, not to get too obsessed with routines, and sleep when I could.

By the time I had Toby, Mat and I were job-sharing. After a short maternity leave, I went back to being a curate half-time. Mat was at home half of the time with Toby and, despite my enjoyment of the baby years, sharing the care with another responsible adult was a great relief. I really enjoyed Toby's baby years. But I still get a slight twinge of jealousy when I come across mothers who seem to have got it all sorted, mothers who say gaily, 'Oh, I love being a mummy at home with my baby!', mothers who fit back into size eight jeans ten minutes after their baby's (natural) birth, mothers who have read and memorized Gina Ford and have their babies in 'routines' by the second week, mothers who sleep – ever.

In today's angst-ridden world where we want to do everything well, where we are used to achieving the highest standards in every other area of our lives, where we are busy and active people who *get things done*, looking after a small, uncooperative creature with a will of its own can come as a huge shock. The reason television programmes like *Supernanny, Little Angels* and *The House of Tiny Tearaways*[6] are so popular is that we want to know how to *do it well*, and we feel guilty if we don't. We too can imagine the stern eyes of Jo Frost looking at us over her horn-rimmed spectacles berating us for 'letting that child rule this home', and we feel it is we who should be on the naughty step, not our children. 'Must try harder', we mutter to ourselves.

I saw an advert in a magazine the other day for the services of a 'parenting coach' – someone who will come to your home for a private consultation to help you to 'effectively manage challenging child behaviour and improve family relationships'.

The fixation with being the perfect parent is not helped by the media obsession with what constitutes a 'bad' parent and the way all the ills of society are blamed on parenting failures:

The cult of individualism, the pressure to earn a living, the desire to rise in a career and the narrative most frequently

---

6. The National Family and Parenting Institute (NFPI) survey found that 72 per cent of 1,000 parents interviewed watched a child-rearing programme; 83 per cent said they found them helpful.

pushed in the popular media that children are a problem and parenting a nightmare, plus the way in which the market's obsession with goals, targets and measurable outcomes has invaded toddlerdom (at 18 months, little Charlotte should be fluent in Mandarin and a senior grade in Budokwai), combine to put enormous hurdles in the way of parents trying to do a good enough job.[7]

Fifty years ago the psychoanalyst Donald Winnicott first aired the idea of the 'good-enough mother'; the mother who wasn't perfect. For Winnicott, the *good-enough* parent was in fact the *very good* parent: parents who did not strive constantly for perfection but let themselves make mistakes, taught their children the important truth that the parent is not all-powerful, but human and flawed, like the rest of the world in which they live. Good-enough parenting is about letting go of perfection. It is not about being lazy or less interested or less loving, but about being more forgiving. It acknowledges that parents, like children, have needs. Each family must find what is important and let the rest slip away. In today's climate of hyperparenting (as I heard someone describe it recently) the concept of the good-enough parent seems to have been drowned out in the cacophony of parenting manuals and 'how to do it properly' TV shows.

Dual-earner families

Juggling two working parents and a family of young children can be a tactical and emotional rollercoaster ride. Or, to use yet another metaphor:

Marriage partners who both hold equally high commitments to work and home life need the agility of an acrobat to meet

7. Yvonne Roberts writing in *Guardian Unlimited*, 15 November 2006, in response to the announcement by Minister for Children Beverley Hughes of the creation of a new National Academy for Parenting Practitioners providing advice on child-rearing techniques.

demands in both arenas. Wanting to do it all, they find that sooner or later something gives. Whether it's work, the marriage, parenting or the emotional health of the acrobats.[8]

Living and working in a dual-earner marriage is a challenge, undoubtedly. For some people it is a burden they would rather not bear but find themselves compelled to do so out of financial obligation. Negative reports of gloom and doom about the effects of both parents working abound. Anne Karpf writes: 'You need two incomes to pay a mortgage. God help you if you have a sick child, a sick parent, or a partner who needs looking after . . . Don't expect the luxury of caring instead of working.'[9]

However, as discussed in the chapter on work and occupation, many women and men *choose* to work and find fulfilment in their lives outside the home. The fact that both parents work does not need to be a bad thing. There are great advantages and benefits to being a dual-earner family. In fact it can be an immense blessing – to both parents, to their children and to the communities in which they live and work. But it takes some doing.

People often ask Mat and me whether one of the problems for us both working in the same field is that we talk about work all the time. We do talk about work a lot, but I would say that this is an advantage rather than a disadvantage. It enables us to empathize with each other, to share concerns and ideas and to feel more in tune with each other. Gilbert's research into dual-earner couples found that on the whole the people involved had higher levels of self-esteem and better overall health than corresponding couples in 'traditional' roles.[10] A study by Silberstein into dual-career couples backs this up. She discovered that couples who talked a lot together about their respective work 'found that this was a means to staying connected with each other'.[11] Interestingly, she found that

8. Judith K. Balswick and Jack O Balswick, 'Marriage as a Partnership of Equals', in Pierce and Groothuis (eds), p. 456.
9. 'Write out 100 times "Rising house prices create latchkey kids"', *Guardian*, 11 November 2006.
10. L.A. Gilbert, 'Two careers/One family: The promise of gender equality' (Sage, 1993), p. 85.
11. L.R. Silberstein, 'Dual Career marriage: a system in transition' (Lawrence Erlbaum Associates, 1992), cited in Walrond-Skinner, *Double Blessing*, p. 57.

couples involved in the same field of work enjoyed even more benefits than those in different fields.

Having both parents working has the potential (and I stress potential) to be advantageous to the well-being of their children also. Provided children are cared for adequately (whether by their parents at different times or by other carers), and provided that their parents spend sufficient time with them, both parents working can bring benefits over and above the financial, especially if the corresponding adjustments are made to enable both parents equally to engage with their children.

By the way, I gave up long ago listening to all the horror stories about what leaving your child in care can do. Both my children have attended nursery and both have benefited from the experience. Good, well-run, caring nurseries can supplement and enhance the experience a child has at home. I remember feeling this one day when I went to pick my daughter up from nursery and found her delightfully messy, covered in spaghetti that her nursery carer had coloured red and with which they were painting pictures. Carer and children were covered from head to toe in red spaghetti and having a brilliant time. I knew I would never in a million years have done something so disgusting and so wonderfully creative at home and I was grateful that someone had done that with her.

Being a dual-earner parent means you need flexibility, good communication with the other parent, a good support network outside the immediate family, a willingness to focus on the things that matter and have standards that are not excessively high in the things that don't. And you need a good sense of humour.

Time pressures

Allow me a brief rant. I can't stand the phrase 'full-time Mum'. You know, when you ask someone what she does for a living and she replies, 'I'm a full-time Mum' (or worse, 'full-time Mummy' – yuk!), by which I assume she doesn't have paid employment outside the home. I always want to reply, 'Well I work outside my home some of the time and I'm a "full-time Mum" too.' Being a mother (or a father) is *always* full-time. I am always a mum whether I am with my children at home cooking them fish fingers or at work giving a seminar. Being a mum is a state, not a job. There is no option to do it full-time or part-time or any other way. There is no sense in which you have 'time off' from being one, or in which you can 'clock off' from being one at the end of the day. What the phrase 'full-time Mum' implies to me is a value judgement that states that the only proper way to be a mother is to be physically with your children for 24 hours a day and to make looking after them your sole occupation. If you work away from them or leave them with anyone else to be looked after you are somehow less of a mother – a 'part-time' one, perhaps. It's not true. Every parent is full-time. That's part of what makes it such an enjoyable, but also such a challenging experience. I'm finished now. Thank you.

Although parenting is always a full-time activity, the perceived lack of time available to spend with our children seems to be the cause of stress for many parents. One survey revealed that a third of people said they didn't have enough time to spend with their families and children.[12] Another revealed that 1.4 million parents in Britain are working regularly through the whole weekend and over 2.5 million families are affected by a parent working regularly over the weekend.[13]

'Family time' is a highly desirable but slightly elusive commodity. I suspect that no one really knows exactly what it means. People resign from high-profile jobs 'in order to spend more time with my family', but what does that mean in practice? Are we referring to long days together or do we mean one day off together a week? Do we mean some time together each day? And even if we decide 'when', do we know 'what'? What should 'time with the family' involve? Is it sitting around an open fire playing board games? Is it eating a meal together? Is it simply being around together at home? I suspect what 'family time' means and how it is

12. Survey by Amicus, Scotland's largest private-sector union, as part of their 'Fair Holiday' campaign. See www.amicustheunion.org.
13. Survey by the National Centre for Social Research, commissioned by Keep Time for Children. See www.keeptimeforchildren.org.uk.

spent will differ from family to family. But that doesn't take away from the fact that there seems to be out there somewhere a utopian standard of what 'enough time with my family' means, which very few parents feel they are reaching properly.

In research carried out by Kerry Daly:[14]

strong tones of obligation entered into many parents' discussion about family time. Often in the same breath, they spoke about the critical importance of family time, and the difficulty of orchestrating it on a regular basis. They wanted the positive togetherness of family time, but often felt too tired after work to deal with all the responsibilities on the home front. In the midst of multiple demands, family time had become something else they should fit into their busy day.

It has long been my view that, despite protestations to the contrary, rather than wanting more family time, some people are actually quite afraid of it. I have a sneaking suspicion (totally unresearched and unproven) that many men (and some women) actually use the long-hours culture at work as an excuse not to come home earlier and spend time with the family. Families are noisy and messy and 'family time' feels like draining hard work sometimes.

'Family time' is a challenge to achieve, not simply because the parents are busy. Whole families are busy. An advertisement for a 'family calendar' appeared on my computer, which said:

Tap dancing on Tuesday, football on Friday, swimming on Saturday . . . these days kids seem to have a better social life than the adults; and Mums and Dads have taken on the unofficial role of taxi drivers! Keep track of the whole family's activities by giving everyone their own column to fill in on the calendar, and life will hopefully feel that little bit less chaotic!

I didn't buy one. I didn't have time.

Children are certainly getting busier. One of the effects of the 'hyperparenting' phenomenon is that it is easy to believe that

14. For the Vanier Institute of the Family in *Transition* magazine, vol. 30, no. 4.

unless you are taking your children to extra classes of gymnastics on a Monday, football on a Tuesday, ballet dancing on a Wednesday, swimming on a Thursday and t'ai chi on a Friday, you are undermining their potential for achievement in later life. Don't get me wrong. There is absolutely nothing wrong with after-school activities and many children enjoy the entertainment and challenge they offer. But there can be an increasing pressure on children to do as much as they can fit in, in order to find acceptance in the busy culture to which they belong.

It's a hard time to be a child. There are many stresses and strains involved. Getting into the right school is one of them, when some schools take attendance at extra curricular activities as evidence of initiative and intelligence in a child and won't accept children who don't do them. Even pre schoolers don't escape the drive to excel. My local leisure centre offers Little Dippers Swimming Lessons, Music with Mummy, Sing and Sign Baby Classes, Parent and Toddler Dance and Music and Tiny Tumblers, just in case your toddler ever gets anywhere near beginning to feel bored. For a second.

A godly perpective

Our images and words for God aren't enough to express fully the nature of God. When God wanted to let us know what he was really like he didn't write words about himself, he sent the 'Word', Jesus – a person not a description. 'The Word became flesh' as it says in John ch. 1. Words are never enough to describe God, but we have to make do with them. God is often described as a 'father' in the biblical text and in the Christian tradition. Using human metaphors like 'Father', 'rock' and 'shepherd' helps us to think about and visualize what God is like in ways that we can understand. The 'fatherhood' of God is a significant and meaningful metaphor. But it is that – a metaphor. And the nature of a metaphor means that there are some ways in which God is like a human father (in being loving, disciplining, caring) and some ways in which God is not like a father. One of the main ways in which God is not like a human father is that he is not male. God is neither male nor female, mother nor father, but God is described as being like a mother, and having the qualities of a mother.

In Isa. 42.14 God describes himself as being like a woman giving birth: 'For a long time I have kept silent, I have been quiet and held myself back. But now, like a woman in childbirth, I cry out, I gasp and pant. I will lay waste the mountains and hills and dry up all their vegetation; I will turn rivers into islands and dry up the pools.'

Many people tend to have an image of God as being rather stern and cross, concerned with how we behave and what we do or don't do, rather than as like a mother who simply wants to love and comfort her child. When my son falls off something, the first thing I do is hold him and comfort him. (I will probably also say 'I told you not to climb up there' afterwards!) The Bible tells us that God longs to hold his people like that, as a mother: 'I will extend prosperity to her like a river, and the wealth of the nations like an overflowing stream; and you shall nurse and be carried on her arm, and dandled on her knees. As a mother comforts her child, so I will comfort you' (Isa. 66.12–13). I have found it very valuable in my own experience of being a mother to know that God identifies with the emotions and experiences of a mother, as well as those of a father.

The Bible teaches that children are neither a right nor an ambition to be fulfilled, but are a gift from God, given to parents who are responsible for their physical, emotional and spiritual upbringing.

It's OK. Don't panic. According to the Bible, children in fact belong to God and their parents are simply the earthly 'trustees' for their care. The Bible understands the role of the parent as history giver: 'We will tell to the coming generation the glorious deeds of the Lord, and his might, and the wonders that he has done' (Ps. 78.4); as rule teacher: 'Keep these words that I am commanding you today in your heart. Recite them to your children and talk about them when you are at home and when you are away, when you lie down and when you rise' (Deut. 6.6–7); as mentor; and as friend.

The experience of hyperparenting teaches us that whatever our children do right is to our credit and whatever they do wrong is our fault. The pressure on parents to mould and influence their children to 'turn out well' is huge and leads to an unattainable perfectionism – another source of stress. Sometimes we can feel that if our children are rude, rebellious and downright rotten, it is somehow our fault for not doing it right, for not doing the right things with them, for not spending enough time with them. The guilt associated with parenting can be huge.

It has always been a great source of encouragement to me that although God is widely held to be the model of a perfect parent, his children are an absolute nightmare. God's children (us) are petulant, rude, disobedient and self-seeking, and yet God is described as being unable to desert them. That is unconditional love in practice. It is evidence that human beings (children included) are created with free will and the capacity to be both glorious and gruesome in equal measure. Which one of those opposites comes to the fore is not necessarily the fault of the parent.

In this area of life more than any other the concept of sacrifice is fundamental. Parenting is in itself a monumental sacrificial act, as you lay down your individuality in order to accommodate another person and love them unconditionally through thick and thin. The first-hand knowledge of such sacrifice is all the more real for parents whose children have not become what their dream for them would have had them be, because of disappointment, illness or – the very worst thing for any parent – the death of a child: 'As parents and children in a modern world that worships individual rights and freedom, nothing is odder than learning to love someone whom we didn't choose.'[15]

If you have children, your devotion to them is important. What is not required of you, however, is to sacrifice *everything* on their behalf. I know too many women who have made gods of their children and an all-consuming vocation of their motherhood. For some people, children and their relationships with them become

---

15. William H. Willimon, 'The people we're struck with', in Adrian Thatcher and Elizabeth Stuart (eds), *Sexuality and Gender* (Gracewing, 1996), p. 173.

the total source of their role, identity, vocation and being and occupy their time completely. There are dangers in this.

One of the most helpful pieces of advice I have been given was from the person who said to me, 'Count yourself as part of the solution'. All too often as parents, and especially, I think, as women, the tendency is to put everyone else's needs before your own. In some ways, this is the Christian thing to do. Yes, we are called to lay down our lives for the good of others, as Jesus did. But Jesus never made himself a doormat to be walked over. He simply carried out his godly vocation. In assessing the needs of our families – in time, in energy, in practical organization, in life choices – it is important that you consider your own needs and your own God-given vocation as part of the equation, as well as the needs of those around you.

Partnership and sacrifice

The changing role of men and parenting

On average, fathers working full-time spend one hour a day on childcare activities during the week and one hour 40 minutes a day at weekends. Full-time working mothers still spend more time on childcare than fathers – two hours a day during the week and two hours 20 minutes a day at weekends.[16] However, there does seem to be an increasing awareness on the part of fathers that if they are not participating fully in the upbringing of their children (and that includes spending plenty of time with them) they, and their kids, are missing out. A poll carried out by YouGov found that 71 per cent of men under 30 said that if it was financially possible they would like to stay at home to look after their children.[17]

Yet, why is it that as I read a feature on the top ten

---

16. Time-use survey undertaken by the Equal Opportunities Commission, quoted on the Economic and Social Research Council website: www.esrc.ac.uk.
17. Cited in Natasha Walter, 'The silence of the fathers is what harms families', *Guardian*, 9 January 2004.

businesswomen in the UK, under each woman's achievements and portfolio of successes is mentioned how many children she has and how she manages to juggle work and home life (several have nannies, two send their children to boarding school and one has a husband who stays at home and looks after them)? You couldn't imagine a similar article about top male business leaders pointing out for our information that 'Mr X has a wife who stays at home and looks after their three small children'! Why is parenting still seen as the responsibility of the woman, when the best model for families is that where mother and father both have an active and involved role in bringing up children and caring for the home?

Writer and 'stay-at-home-Dad' Steve Cochrane writes of his constantly being told how marvellous he is just because he is doing what many women do all the time without comment, that is, working from home and looking after his small children: 'If women want men to take more of an active hand in the raising of children, and I'm sure they do, then they ought to start treating the relatively few who do in the same way as they treat all the other mums they meet.'[18]

Mat likewise often had the experience of being looked at rather strangely every time he was the only bloke at the toddler group or the only dad picking kids up from the school gate. The expectation still seems to be that caring for children is *really* women's work. I recall a time when I had to go away for a weekend as part of my work. The children and Mat stayed at home. A friend of ours asked beforehand, 'Will Mat be OK with that? Is there anything I can do to help?' Mat found himself replying through slightly gritted teeth: 'No, it's OK. I'm sure I'll manage. I am their father after all.'

One of the answers to today's busyness issue for families is for fathers to take more of an active role in caring for their children, and for women simultaneously to stop feeling guilty about not being 'there for them' every minute God sends. Natasha Walter agrees:

> The crunch question of our times, about how to preserve family life against the pressures of the workplace, cannot be solved by women making each other feel guilty about going to work. It

18. Steve Cochrane, 'Saint Dad', *Guardian*, 27 July 2005.

could, however, be solved by men making each other feel guilty about refusing to abandon long hours in the workplace. They, too, should learn to spend some years letting promotion pass them by as they do another kind of work, the kind that is irreplaceable to those who love them.[19]

The case for co-parenting

Sharing parenting is well documented to provide benefits for the children concerned:

> An accumulation of evidence demonstrates the benefits of co-parenting to children and parents alike. When father and mother are jointly involved in parenting, a strong parental partnership enhances their leadership capacity. Together and separately, a mother and father can nurture as well as teach, equip, disciple and give wise counsel.[20]

Co-parenting also helps with busyness, because the task can be shared. It is never assumed that the life, work and tasks that one parent has to achieve are more important than the life, work and tasks of the other. Who does what is arrived at by discussion and negotiation (and common sense and reality) rather than a 'the children are your responsibility' default position.

So far, our two seem to be fairly normal kids, with the same hang-ups, strengths and accomplishments as most other kids I know. But I like to believe that the co-parenting they have experienced will stand them in good stead to be confident and competent adults. They have both seen examples of a strong mother and a nurturing father, a caring mother and an ambitious father, a fulfilled mother and a gentle father, a tender mother and a motivated father. They have also seen a stressed mother and a cross

19. Walter, 'The silence of the fathers is what harms families'.
20. Diane Ehrensaft, *Parenting Together: Men and women sharing the care of their children* (University of Illinois Press, 1990), cited in Balswick and Balswick, 'Marriage as a partnership of equals', p.454.

father, a frustrated mother and tired father, but only some of the time. The point is that they have seen examples of femininity and masculinity in just about equal measure. They know what it is to be female and male, and our hope is that our daughter will grow into a 'feminine woman' and our son into a 'masculine man'. But they have also seen that the task of nurturing and loving is not exclusive to the woman, nor is the task of breadwinning and leading exclusive to the man. Our hope is that they will have the confidence to be whatever they are called by God to be in later life, not what gender stereotypes might wish to restrict them to.

It is surprising how strong those cultural messages can be, even in today's so-called 'egalitarian' society. I cringe every time I see adverts that state things like 'That's why mums shop at [insert name of major frozen food retailer here]' or the advert for a brand of baby bath that chimes: 'When a baby is born, so is a mother.' What happened to the fathers? Children very easily imbibe stereotypical ideas about gender from the world around them. All the careful and consistent modelling of gender equality Mat and I have done didn't stop Toby from turning to me as I told him off about something the other day and saying, 'You can't tell me off, because daddy is in charge!'

Parenting is intended to be a partnership between men and women. The Bible teaches the importance of both parents' involvement in the lives of their children. Nowhere does Scripture teach that mothering is more important than fathering. In order to raise a child well, the input, love and care of both male and female are needed. The ideal is of a mother and a father living together and caring together in equal measure for their children, but as we have seen throughout this section the ideal is rarely accomplished, and we live very much in the real world, especially where marriage and children are concerned. Sometimes we just have to learn to live with imperfection and trust in the amazing ability of God to redeem situations that the world around us would see as unpromising.

A note for people who do not live with the father or mother of their children. It is still possible to co-parent, even at a distance. In fact the child who spends some time with mum and some time with dad may experience co-parenting better than the child who lives with both in traditional roles where dad goes out to work and mum is on hand all the time. When you only have your kids for the weekend, you spend every minute with them, you care for them and cook for them and clean for them and talk to them. They see both parents doing all the things parents can do.

I grew up from 11 onwards with parents who didn't live together and I really appreciated the time I spent at home with my mum but also the weekends and holidays I spent at my dad's house. One of my most vivid memories of this time is cooking with my dad, grating the cheese for a cauliflower cheese we were making together. In my mind, men and women have always been able to cook equally well, and shop, and clean and work and look after children.

If you don't have contact with the father or mother of your child for whatever reason, it is possible and advisable to find substitute, balancing role models of maleness and femaleness – uncles, aunts, youth club leaders, Sunday school teachers, grandparents, friends.

Co-parenting doesn't need to be a complete life change. If you are in a lifestyle where one of you goes out to work full-time and the other is at home with small children, things are bound to get a bit unequal in the parenting arena, or at least the practical side of it. But you can still develop attitudes of co-parenting in this: making sure you get home early enough after work to do some of the hands-on aspects of parenting. Yes, that will involve making sacrifices at work. Making sure you spend good amounts of time with your children at weekends and in the holidays. And if you do get the chance to job-share, or really to choose jobs and ways of living that allow you equal time with your kids, don't hesitate to do it.

Stepping above

The following are some tips for parenting in the busyness.

Don't do it alone

Bringing up a child is not meant to be a solitary task. There is an African proverb that says, 'It takes a village to raise a child'. It means that raising a child well takes the love and care of not just parents but the whole community, all of whom have a role in bringing up its children.

Although women are spending more time in the workplace, they are still in many families responsible for most of the work at home. If this is the case in your home, open up a discussion on sharing the workload. Whether you're a mother who finds that the responsibility for parenting falls mostly on your shoulders, and you need to sit down and have an honest talk with your partner about what he might do. Whether you are a single parent who needs to enlist the help of some good friends or family to support you in your parenting. Whether you are a working parent who needs to stop feeling guilty about taking your child to a nursery or child-minder. Each of us needs to hear the message that we are not meant to go it alone.

Christian community can provide a good source of support in the task of raising children. I would not have survived my first year as a mother without some well-run baby and toddler groups and a couple of older women from my church who looked after me. One of the main advantages we found living in the Lee Abbey community for four years while our children were small was the constant support and companionship that was provided in the task of parenting; however, living as part of a community also means your parenting skills or otherwise are constantly on show – there is no hiding your child's table manners when you're eating with 100 others. There were other families in the community to whom we could turn for advice or a cup of tea when things got rough. There were wonderful role models in the form of young Christian men and women whom our children could look to as a source of inspiration. One of the things I valued most was the good relationship our son had with the younger men who would play football with him. There were members who led a 'cell group' for the community children to nurture them in their faith. Best of all was having 100 on-tap babysitters!

What life in community at Lee Abbey taught us was that although 'time as a family' is important, there is also the need for 'community time', when people other than yourselves have an input into the life and development of your children. It is not as easy in a church to re-create the physical, emotional, spiritual and practical closeness of a community like Lee Abbey, but the principle of shared responsibility for the well-being of the children in a community is one that could be increasingly embraced in the local church too.

Redeem the time you have

Instead of feeling guilty about the time you *don't* spend with your children, make the most of the time you *do* have together. 'Family time' should be time that is well spent and beneficial for both children and parents, not something that is done 'because I ought to' but because I want to and I enjoy it.

Perhaps with busy schedules and multiple responsibilities we have to be more purposeful in making time for our families. This may mean setting aside time each week for a family activity or meal. But do things you all enjoy rather than things you feel should be necessarily instructive or educational.

Routines can be terribly important. Children respond well to a sense of consistency and regularity in the midst of a hectic schedule. Bedtime routines are particularly important. We have always refused work between teatime and when the children are in bed (although that's becoming harder as our elder child stays up later now). But being there for bath time as far as possible, having a good routine where you read to or with children before they go to bed – these can be precious moments. Walking your children to school is a great opportunity to talk together. We walk both of our children to school and although it is often 'inconvenient' I wouldn't miss that shared time for anything in the world. My daughter will happily talk about her day on the way home from school but once she gets through the front door she prefers to leave the world of school behind her; she clams up and won't talk about it any more. Without that ten minutes of catching up as we walk home, I doubt I would hear much about how her day has gone. My son talks all the way to school and all the way back, usually about cars. Yesterday he was telling me about a scheme he has devised to make sure all the poor people in the world will be able to afford Ferraris.

Be available

Being available might mean being there enough to turn quantity time into quality time. It is often after 19 fairly mundane conversations walking home from school with Molly that the twentieth more significant revelation will pop up. Being available might mean being there at key times. It might mean making family life a priority. As with marriage, your calling is to be a parent, above your work.

We are faced with an abundance of choices, and it's easy to get caught up in doing too much. If you sense your family life getting too busy simply to enjoy each other's company, consider cutting back on activity. Instead of always rushing children off to scheduled activities, stay at home sometimes and just relax together. One of the most valuable things we can do for our children is simply to 'waste time' with them. In our busy lives where time is a precious commodity, doing 'nothing very much' with your children speaks volumes about how you see them and the value you place on your relationship. Spending Saturday afternoons gardening together, making a cake together, just slobbing about on the sofa watching TV together – all of this is time well spent.

I told my daughter I was writing about being a good mum or dad even when you're busy and asked her what her advice would be for busy parents who wanted to do a good job with their children. Her response was simple: 'Do stuff together.'

Model values

Train children in the right way, and when old, they will not stray. (Prov. 22.6)

Be an example to your children. Values are important and children pick up values from what they observe you doing, often unintentionally, as much as from what you set out to do deliberately. So seeing both their parents active and fulfilled and happy is an important visual lesson for children. That does not mean you need to be perfect, but be aware of what you model, especially in the area of gender relating.

Being an example for your children does not mean that they only see the good bits. We are human, warts and all, and if our children are to learn to be fully human too they must see us express the full range of human emotions. I don't worry when our children see us having an argument. I never saw my parents argue and as a result I find it quite hard to deal with conflict myself. If they see us arguing, it's also important that they see us make up afterwards. Let them see you expressing your affection for each other. Let them see you sad and tell them why (if appropriate, of course). We can never be perfect but we can use the mistakes we make by admitting them and asking for forgiveness from our children. Children need to learn how to make mistakes and learn from them as well as how to do it right. They pick a lot up from our actions and responses to things – both positive and negative – but they don't always know what to make of them until later in life. Children need to learn to think for themselves out of their own owned personal beliefs, which can be modelled for them in the early years. This includes modelling Christian faith, if that is what is important to you.

Above all, children need modelled for them parents who are available, have time for them and actually quite like them.

Having a little rest 9

Leisure, home and hospitality

God's intention was not that human beings should work every hour he sends, but that they should find time to rest.

Sabbath for busy people

When God had finished his work of creation, he rested:

> Thus the heavens and the earth were finished, and all their multitude. And on the seventh day God finished the work that he had done, and he rested on the seventh day from all the work that he had done. So God blessed the seventh day and hallowed it, because on it God rested from all the work that he had done in creation. (Gen. 2.1–3)

What was good enough for God was good enough for God's people and the command to observe a Sabbath rest was a key part of God's guidelines for healthy people, healthy communities and healthy society: 'For six days you shall do your work, but on the seventh day you shall rest, so that your ox and your donkey may have relief, and your home-born slave and the resident alien may be refreshed' (Exod. 23.12). I don't see many home-born slaves around my area of Bristol and resident aliens have taken on a whole new meaning in most people's minds, but the principle still stands. Rest is important. Sabbath literally means 'stop' and that is exactly what God intends that we should do sometimes – stop.

If only it was that easy.

Today, rest has to be quick and efficient. Tim Chester talks about the phenomenon of 'binge resting', where we work like stink for 50 weeks of the year in order to take an intensive two-week holiday in the summer.[1] Our rest time, rather than incorporated into the whole of our lives, becomes a short, sharp burst that has questionable benefits. In Japan, there are small, inexpensive booths in city-centre hotels into which busy office workers can climb for a few hours' rest before going back to work the next day. It is now a virtue to get by on as little sleep as possible.

These days, even leisure time has become very active. We are meant to have more leisure time than ever, with reasonable holiday entitlements and working-time directives. But it doesn't feel like that. Leisure time has become less 'what we use to relax' and more 'what we use to get things done'. Po Bronson, writing in *Time* magazine, identifies the concept of 'active leisure': 'Anytime you exhaust yourself trying to relax, that's "active leisure".'[2] Many people are so active in their leisure that it adds to their stress, instead of reducing it.

This throws up the whole question about what is leisure anyway, and what is relaxing? What one person considers relaxing another considers boring. Personality has to come into it somewhere. The other day I had what many would consider to be 'a day off'. I was not writing or speaking or working in any way. I had no set plans. But it was one of the busiest days I had that week. I spent the morning cleaning the house. I took the dog out for a walk. I cooked a cake with my five-year-old son. (I know. Can you see my halo?) I took my daughter to her friend's house for a sleepover. I wrote some letters, answered some emails, phoned my mother, then cooked a nice meal for my husband and me, and finally settled down to watch a film, at about 9 p.m. And that's leisure? The thing is, I really enjoyed my day. All of those things I did relax and energize me. They are the things I would choose to

1. Tim Chester, *The Busy Christian's Guide to Busyness* (IVP, 2006).
2. 'Just sit back and relax!', *Time* magazine, 26 June 2006.

do with my 'spare' time. Yet it was another busy day. Is that wrong? Is that Sabbath, or is it more stress? What do we do to rest and recuperate these days? What makes our spare time so busy? When even relaxation is 'active', how can real rest be found? Is there still room for 'Sabbath' in today's culture?

The Sabbath *principle* is that for one day a week, or for a certain period of time regularly, we are to stop, rest and be refreshed as God was. The common assumption is that the Sabbath time is that time when you don't work. For some, that's the weekend, but now even the weekend has become a time of busyness, where all the things we don't have time to do during a hectic Monday–Friday get pushed into the time on Saturday/Sunday. If Sabbath is simply a time when you don't have to work, it doesn't apply very easily to people who work from home, or people who are unemployed, or parents at home with small children. There are more questions than ever to be asked of our 'time of rest'.

The whole concept of Sabbath has been damaged by a some-times Pharisaic insistence that Sabbath must be on one particular day, and that day must be a Sunday. There are, of course, benefits to any society of having one day where there is generally and communally not as much activity as on the other days of the week. But to be adamant that Sabbath must happen for everyone on Sunday, when everything must stop, is to miss the point. Indeed, many people of older generations speak of the consummate boredom that Sunday held, when you weren't allowed to do anything fun, when nothing was open, no one could do anything (except go to church) and the clock ticked very slowly and quietly through the day. That's not Sabbath, that's torture!

What you do in your Sabbath times is a matter for individual choice. The time we take for our Sabbath will be different. Robert Warren and Sue Mayfield, in their Lent study on the principles of Sabbath, *Life Attitudes*, say that Sabbath may be expressed in whole days, moments, attitudes and seasons. And what we do with it may be different too. Your Sabbath may be very different from my Sabbath. Jesus spoke of this freedom to interpret the Sabbath in a way that brought life rather than limitation and restriction when he said, 'The Sabbath was made for humankind, and not humankind for the Sabbath' (Mk 2.27).

Sabbath is an attitude rather than a rule of law. The attitude it reflects is that it is not good to be occupied with hard work and productivity all the time. It is good to do things that relax and rejuvenate you, your family and your community. Sabbath is more about refreshment, reflection, justice, giving, freedom, restoration, relaxation, life than it is about not doing certain things. It is that inner rest that energizes us for the work God calls us each to do. Sabbath is a chance to step above the clamour of everyday life, but it may be a time of activity, if that activity is for you refreshing, invigorating and life-giving. Several writers have talked about the 'Sabbath of the heart', finding ways to rest that are appropriate for you. If you're an active person, you might not benefit from being told that all you need to do is stop. For you, that might be stressful and decidedly unrelaxing. Rest might mean doing something busy but creative, something that you choose to do that is different from what you normally do. If you're a lively, bouncy person, the worst thing in the world might be to be still and quiet. Shouting your head off in a football stadium or raving all night at a club might be your idea of refreshment. The introvert will need space alone, the extrovert other people to be with, and so on.

The basic necessities of human living include sleep, food and shelter, but how do we find time to attend properly to these things in a culture where time is the most precious commodity? This chapter explores some of the bare necessities of life and home, analysing the different voices we are hearing about the way we look, the way our homes look, how fit we are and what we can 'achieve' in our leisure time. The key is to enable us as busy people to put in the basic building blocks of healthy living, so that we might thrive in the midst of the action – and find rest for our souls.

Messages

Sleep

In our busy lives, sleep is possibly the one activity (can you call it that?) we do that makes us totally stop. While we're sleeping we can't actually do anything else. In sleep, the stresses and strains of a busy day grow dim and find perspective. Sleep is refreshing, healing, calming and nourishing: in fact, all the things most sought after in a busy, non-stop, stressful culture. I still remember from school-days the wonderfully evocative description of sleep in Shakespeare's *Macbeth*: 'Sleep that knits up the ravell'd sleeve of care,/The death of each day's life, sore labour's bath,/Balm of hurt minds, great nature's second course,/Chief nourisher in life's feast.' Sleep is a good thing. But it's hard to find time to do enough of it.

If time is at a premium, the currency many people use to pay for it is their sleep time. 'Sleep in our over-busy culture has become infinitely reducible, the only truly expendable deadline. Sleep has to fill the time left over from everything else.'[3] And when 'everything else' amounts to a great deal, the time for sleep is dramatically reduced. If you can survive on five hours a night, why not? 'If it was good enough for Margaret Thatcher, it is good enough for me', we say.

The problem with this pushing of sleep to the end of the To Do List is that, over time, there is a discernible effect on the quality of life of most people who try to live like this. Sleep deprivation can cause mental and physical deterioration. Scientific studies at the University of Chicago have shown that sleep-deprived rats 'died within two or three weeks, having first become increasingly debilitated, developed sores, lost weight despite eating more than usual, and suffered a drop in body temperature'.[4] Even though the outcome might not be quite as dramatic as death, it's not just rats that are affected. Women who sleep less than five hours a night, we are told, are at an 82 per cent increased risk of heart attack. I have a friend, a busy working mother, who regularly cleans her house at 1 a.m., sleeps for three or four hours a night and when you have her over for a meal, usually falls asleep at the dinner table.

The Bible talks about sleep as being designed by God for human health and refreshment. Sleep is not earned but is a gift from God, emanating from his loving heart: 'It is in vain that you rise up early and go late to rest, eating the bread of anxious toil; for he gives

3. Anne Karpf, *Guardian*, 11 February 2006.
4. 'And so to bed', *The Economist*, 19 December 2002.

sleep to his beloved' (Ps. 127.2). Sleep is part of the pattern of living, as well as pointing to the sustaining hand of God on the life of the sleeper: 'I lie down and sleep; I wake again, for the Lord sustains me' (Ps. 3.5). The ability to sleep anyway in the midst of the hubbub of life, despite it all, even though there's no time for it, even though it's inconvenient, signals the complete trust of the sleeper in the hands of God to save and protect while defences are down. The ultimate example of this kind of trust is shown by Jesus as he sleeps in the boat in the middle of a raging storm, much to the consternation of the terrified disciples (Mt. 8.23–25).

When things get too busy and I get stressed about all I have to do, it keeps me awake at night. I lie there in the small hours worrying about what I have to do the next day, and wondering how it will all fit. The wisdom literature of Proverbs and Ecclesiastes paints a picture of a person who is able to sleep comfortably because of their trust in God and their obedience to his statutes: 'If you sit down, you will not be afraid; when you lie down, your sleep will be sweet. Do not be afraid of sudden panic, or of the storm that strikes the wicked; for the Lord will be your confidence and will keep your foot from being caught' (Prov. 3.24–26).

However, over-dependence on sleep, or laziness, is seen as folly in the Bible: 'Do not love sleep, or else you will come to poverty; open your eyes, and you will have plenty of bread' (Prov. 20.13). In God's ideal, labour and rest, work and sleep must be held in balance. Too much of one or the other is likely to lead to an imbalance in well-being.

The need for godly balance also applies to the way we look, the food we eat and the way we treat our bodies.

Bodies

There is a cultural battle raging over the way we view our bodies – what shape they are, what we feed them, what we dress them in.

On the one hand you are confronted with the cult of celebrity – unless you are as skinny as Victoria Beckham, as toned as Paula Radcliffe, as well dressed as Kate Moss and as wealthy as Paris

Hilton, it's really not worth your while getting out of bed in the morning. (That's just the women, obviously. For men substitute Johnny Depp, Shane Warne, David Beckham and Brad Pitt.) On the other hand there is an increased obsession with food – more choice about what and where to eat, more restaurants, more cooking programmes. Jamie Oliver is lauded as the saviour of British children for his campaign to introduce healthy food into school dinner menus – then berated for restricting the choice of the little darlings and held responsible for the falling revenues of school dinner providers as kids opt out of the healthy option in favour of the chip shop and packed lunches.

On the one hand there is an obsession with being fit and toned and on the other hand there is more and more entertainment that will keep you firmly planted on the sofa – Xboxes, multi-channel cable and satellite TV, computer games.

What about where we live? On the one hand we watch programmes like *Home*, *House Doctor*, *Grand Designs* and *Extreme House Makeover* and yearn for the beautiful interiors we see there. On the other hand we are living in a society where houses prices are more exorbitant than ever, where the average house price in many areas is ten times the average annual salary[5] and where many people can't even afford to repair their guttering, let alone install a tasteful cast-iron spiral staircase.

It's all very confusing, and ever so slightly frustrating.

Looking at the life of Jesus apparently doesn't really help a great deal either. What could a first-century nomadic man possibly tell us about fashion, food and fitness? Jesus's own teaching about the physical, practical side of life was fairly unambiguous. We are not to concern ourselves excessively with these things: 'Therefore I tell you, do not worry about your life, what you will eat or what you will drink, or about your body, what you will wear. Is not life more than food, and the body more than clothing? Look at the birds of the air; they neither sow nor reap nor gather into barns,

---

5. A report published in May 2006 by the National Housing Federation shows that average house prices in England rose to almost eight times the average salary in 2005. House prices have increased by 125 per cent since 1997, but incomes have gone up by just 18 per cent in the same period.

and yet your heavenly Father feeds them. Are you not of more value than they?' (Mt. 6.25–26).

Jesus's apparent lack of concern with body, clothes, food, sleep or shelter might lead us to think they should not concern us either. Certainly, there is a need to put things like fashion and faddism into perspective, as we will see. On a relative scale perhaps we should concern ourselves more with eternal issues such as life, death, love, justice and the coming of God's kingdom on earth. However, the overall biblical imperative is that we should take care of ourselves, our bodies and our homes. Actually, the Bible as a whole has a great deal of helpful insight into how we should live physically as well as spiritually, much of it as applicable today as when it was written.

Food

One of the most popular television programmes of the past few years in the UK is called *You Are What You Eat*. Its presenter Gillian McKeith (described on the Channel 4 website as a 'straight-talking holistic nutritionist') performs a kind of foodie makeover on the fridge contents and eating habits of 'Britain's worst eaters'. It is just one of a whole raft of programmes and publications aimed at helping busy people today to cook well and eat healthily. If we are so in love with cooking and eating, why do we have such an uneasy relationship with food?

If Britain is what it eats, it is at the same time overfed (during the last 25 years, the rate of obesity has quadrupled in the UK[6]) and starving itself (the Eating Disorders Association has estimated that at least one million people in the UK are affected by anorexia and bulimia – as many as one woman in 20 has some form of eating problem)[7].

Food, like sleep and exercise, is meant to be good, life-giving, enjoyable – the ideal counter to a stressful and busy life. Surely food, and the sharing of it with other people, should be something that is an integral, glorious aspect of life that sustains individuals,

6. Economic and Social Research Council, www.esrc.ac.uk.
7. www.edauk.com

preserves families and builds community. One of the needs in the busyness is to take another look at this most vital of life's activities and to find out how food might be a source of refreshment, energy and community, as God intended.

Nigella Lawson is one of my heroes. Not only is she exceptionally beautiful (but in a realistic, rounded, womanly way), she is a fabulous cook and a very clever businesswoman, as well as being a wife and mum. The thing I appreciate about her most, though, is her attitude to food. In a culture obsessed with food, eating either too much of it or not enough, Nigella sees food as something to be celebrated, as part of real life with all its joy and pain. She has had more than her fair share of loss in her own life, watching her mother, her sister and her first husband die early of cancer, and yet her attitude is that food is there to sustain, comfort and feast upon, even when life is very difficult. In the introduction to her cookery book *Feast: Food that celebrates life*, she says: 'How we eat and what we eat lies at the heart of who we are – as individuals, families, communities ... Basic to the whole thing of being human is that we use food to mark occasions that are important to us in life. It's how we mark the connections between us, how we celebrate life.'[8] More than simply being 'what we eat', we are also 'how we eat'. One of the most valuable activities that can be undertaken is eating with other people.

A book was published in 2002 asking the question *What Would Jesus Eat?* The book is described by its author Don Colbert (a Californian doctor) in the back-cover blurb as 'offering all the information you need for good eating, good exercising and good living'. (The answer to the question by the way is 'lots of vegetables, especially beans and lentils, wheat bread, a lot of fruit, a lot of water and also red wine'.)[9] You could even buy the *What Would Jesus Eat Cookbook* which contains a lovely recipe for olive oil dressing, amongst other things. The book was widely pilloried in the UK as another example of American literalism gone mad. Of course we can never really know what Jesus ate, and why should our speculation determine what we eat in today's vastly different

8. *Nigella Lawson, Feast: Food that celebrates life* (Chatto and Windus, 2004), p. vii.
9. Don Colbert, *What Would Jesus Eat?* (STL, 2002).

world anyway? Dr Colbert, however, makes some interesting points about the *way* we eat in comparison to the way people ate in biblical times: 'They would eat for hours and take their time. The disciples would be lounging around and conversing while dining, not eating fast food on the go like we do.'[10]

We live in a fast-food culture that allows us to grab food on the go, often alone – at a tube station kiosk on the way to a meeting, on our laps in front of the TV – ready-prepared food that is microwaveable in minutes. This is all well and good to some extent, and I like a good pre-packaged sandwich as well as the next person. But there is something lost in continually snatching food and eating it alone, rather than preparing and savouring it with others, simply because we are too busy to take the time to 'eat properly'.

There is a very real sense today in which we are what we eat – fast, frantic and rushed. The philosopher and writer Roger Scruton expresses this in an article about the way we eat today:

> Food is the place where the needs of the body and the needs of the soul converge, to offer nourishment and meaning in equal measure. If there is to be criticism of the fast-food culture it surely lies here: that it denies our need for meaning, not merely by addressing appetite alone, not merely by its bland uniformity of presentation, content and aesthetic, but by its conscious detachment from place, community and ceremony. In the fast-food culture food is not given but taken ... The solitary stuffing of burgers, pizzas and 'TV dinners'; the disappearance of family meals and domestic cooking; the loss of table manners – all these tend to obscure the distinction between eating and feeding.[11]

What has been forfeited in all the busyness is a sense that food is about offering and loving, giving and nourishing, rather than simply eating and getting full. The way we eat our food is one of the things that makes us most human.

10. Colbert, quoted in Michelle Roberts, 'Americans look to Jesus for diet', www.newsbbc.co.uk (23 May 2005).
11. 'Eating the world: the philosophy of food' (2003) on the Open Democracy website: www.opendemocracy.net.

One of the most relaxing things I do is make bread. I buy bread from a shop too, but on the occasions that I take the time to make a loaf of bread there is the feeling of doing something very basic, almost primal. In the kneading of the dough and the shaping of the loaf there is a sense in which I am truly providing for my family: 'Give us this day our daily bread . . .'

Mat and I have always had a hard and fast rule that we eat our evening meal together, with our children, as a family. Before we were ordained, when Mat was working as an engineer, he used to go to work early so he could leave earlier and be home in time to eat together. When we went to theological college, we stubbornly refused to go to anything, meetings, events or lectures that happened at teatime. In the parish for our curacy we would never arrange meetings, go visiting or do anything else between the hours of 5 and 7.30, unless it was a dire emergency. At Lee Abbey, we stipulated before we joined the community that we would want to eat together at home as a family for our evening meal, rather than joining with the guests and other community. It has not always been easy to stick to. At times it has felt to be an unpopular decision with colleagues and others. It has become an almost religious crusade for us to set aside this time as a family each evening to sit around a table together and eat. It's not always been a time of joy and harmony. Our kids have sometimes squabbled and been rude, and refused to eat what we ate. Yet now that our children are growing older, our zeal for family teatime has begun to bear fruit. It has become the best time of our day to talk together. We enjoy each other's company. We laugh a lot. The kids (far from being perfect in their eating habits) will generally eat most of what is put in front of them and both of them have surprisingly mature tastes for so-called 'adult' foods like olives and mustard and curry. I'm not saying that our mealtimes resemble some kind of happy, hazy image from an Oxo advert. What I am saying, though, is that the decision to eat a communal meal together as a family, as a couple, as friends, as regularly as is humanly possible, is a decision you are very unlikely to regret – no matter how busy you get.

Now I know it won't work for everyone every day. Some people simply get home too late from work to eat with their children every night. But even a weekly meal together can go a long way towards building family life and nurturing relationships. A lot can be achieved around a dinner table. In an age where fewer and fewer homes have communal dining tables and fewer and fewer families eat together regularly,[12] the decision to sit down together and eat now more than ever signals a desire to live life differently, by different standards.

Jamie Oliver, the celebrity chef (in one description: 'the larky lad about town, grown-up daddy, businessman and chef with a social conscience'), agrees: 'I might be biased, but I think if you got everyone to eat round the table two or three times a week, you'd get a drop in the divorce rate. And as for kids, they might not know it yet, but they'll thank their parents when they get older.'[13]

Eating together is a biblical theme. The first major event in the Bible was a shared snack. OK, so Eve giving the forbidden fruit to Adam isn't the best example of communal eating, but shows that food certainly has an essential role in the biblical narrative. God is a hospitable God who invites us to sit and eat with him: 'You embraced us as your children and welcomed us to sit and eat with you.'[14] It is in God's character to offer hospitality. Psalm 23 paints the picture of God setting up a meal for his beloved followers: 'You prepare a table before me in the presence of my enemies. You anoint my head with oil; my cup overflows.'

From the hospitality of Abraham at the oaks of Mamre to the final wedding banquet at the end of time, the Bible is stuffed full of food – and of people eating it together. Throughout Jesus's ministry we see him eating with his disciples and friends, as well as with outcasts. In sharing a meal with tax collectors and sinners, Jesus signals his love and acceptance of them, against cultural and societal norms (Lk. 15.1–2). He uses mealtimes in his teaching as allegories for the kingdom of God (Mt. 22.1–14) and he describes himself as the 'bread of life' (Jn 6.35). Jesus left his disciples with the

---

12. According to the 2004 National Family Mealtime Survey, 20 per cent of those asked sat down to eat together once a week or less (www.raisingkids.co.uk). The latest figures show that only 64 per cent of teenagers in Britain regularly sit down to a meal with their parents.

13. Interview for *Good Housekeeping* magazine, November 2006.

14. Eucharistic prayer H from *Common Worship* (Church House Publishing, 2000).

instruction that they were to 'do this in remembrance of me' (Lk. 22.19). What is 'this'? Essentially, eating a meal together. The Eucharist, or shared communal meal celebrated in every Christian church and community, is the central act of the Christian life and witness which not only provides spiritual focus but also sustains and nurtures the community:

> Meals are especially privileged moments of the intimate presence because of the reality of caring and sharing they entail. Their intimate presence is irreplaceable in a society of high mobility ... It is like a natural sacrament of love and life which supports family communication and points in faith to the agape of the eucharist.'[15]

I love hosting dinner parties – deciding what to cook, shopping for ingredients, preparing, cooking, laying the table, getting things ready and then feeding people when they come to my table, not only with food, but also with conversation, acceptance and hospitality. I vividly recall the moment, the day after I was ordained priest, when I presided at Communion for the first time. Standing behind the table, getting it all ready, inviting people to come, it struck me very clearly then that I was hosting a meal – I was providing hospitality at God's table. That feeling has remained with me ever since, every time I celebrate with others the Lord's Supper. Sometimes, if it's appropriate, I bake the bread too. There is something very special about blessing the bread your own hands have made – and then offering it to others as food for their journeys.

Every time we offer hospitality, every time we provide a meal, every time we eat with others, every time we break bread together, we are doing something godly, offering something of ourselves, making space for others, providing safety, shelter, refreshment, relationship and rest. It's worth making time for.

---

15. German Martinez, 'Marriage as worship: A theological analogy', in Thatcher and Stuart (eds), *Sexuality and Gender*, p. 188.

Fitness

As with food and sleep, the drive for health and fitness is both something we don't pay enough attention to in our society and are obsessed with in about equal measure.

Scientific research shows that regular exercise cuts dramatically the risk of diseases such as heart attack, stroke, diabetes and a whole host of other health risks. Five sessions per week of moderate exercise of about 30 minutes' duration each is the current advice. We also live in a culture that is obsessed with looks, body image and 'being toned'. Research suggests that around one in five people in the UK is a regular user of a health club or leisure centre. Over the past decade there has been an explosion in the launch of new health and fitness clubs. In an industry which is believed to be worth some £1.3 billion, there are now over 4,500 members' clubs.

The health-club culture holds a great appeal for many people. In a society where community is sought after, yet feared, belonging to 'your' gym, where other members are 'people like you', holds a certain appeal. The gym offers a context in which to make friendships, but in a safe, acceptable and controllable environment, as you talk to someone on the treadmill, or share a quick drink at the health-club bar. In fact, many people go to their gym for similar reasons to those which used to take them to church – ritual (albeit on a treadmill), discipline (albeit physical rather than spiritual), community (albeit 'members-only') and the opportunity to feel that you're doing something 'good'. It is no coincidence that many health-club chains have vaguely spiritual-sounding names, such as The Third Space and Living Well.

Fitness has become something else you have to squeeze into your already pressured time. So you don't just go to the gym, you dash to the gym and get fit quickly. I saw a sign outside a gym in my area advertising, not just 'exercise', but 'fast, efficient, effective exercise'! Sounds exhausting. The latest device to hit the fitness world is the VibroGym, a kind of vibrating platform on which the exerciser stands to perform their fitness routine. It looks like an instrument of torture, but the advertising hype tells us that 'The VibroGym is fast and effective. Maximum results are achieved in a minimum of time, with no extra stress and only limited effort.' It's no longer good enough simply to exercise. Now you have to exercise *quickly*!

One of the things Lee Abbey is good at is cake. A couple of months after we joined the community I realized I had put on a stone in weight, simply through eating the cake that was provided (lovingly of course) at every teatime by the kitchen team. I lived with that quite happily for a while, but then decided that I was hurtling with alarming alacrity towards 40 and that if I didn't shape up now, I never would. The bits that were already descending southwards would continue to do so until I was saggy all over. I didn't want this to happen. At least, not yet. So I decided to lose some weight and get fit. The two went together. For me it was important that this wasn't just about dieting, but about developing healthy patterns of eating and exercising. I set about it with vigour and with the help of some fairly strict cutting down on fatty food (especially cake) and a three-times-a-week jigging about in my living-room to Rosemary Conley's fat-busting fitness video, I managed to lose a stone and a half. I could also begin to see that underneath it all I had muscles! I liked the new way I looked. So did my husband. And I've kept it up a year and a half on. Now I don't tell you this because I am in any way a paragon of health and fitness virtue. It's just that I feel so much better. I hear so many of my friends tell me they're too busy to do regular exercise. In many ways I sympathize. It is very difficult to fit in a regular trip to the gym or the swimming pool when your work keeps you in an office from 9 to 6. However, the benefits that exercise brings are really too great for it to be pushed to the back of the queue.

There are ways of exercising that don't involve an hour a day on a treadmill. A brisk walk to work is one of the best forms of exercise you can do, as is pushing a pushchair around a park, as is cycling to church, as is playing a round of golf, or whatever. A recent report has shown that one of the best things you can do to get fit is get a dog. A study by the University of Portsmouth's Department of Environmental Design and Management has found that the UK's 6.2 million dogs help motivate their 15 million owners by encouraging them to exercise through a daily walk, even when they don't feel like it. As a family we talked endlessly for a couple of years about whether to get a dog. For a long while the argument went that we were too busy to walk one. One day, however, and after a lot of nagging by our daughter, we came to the conclusion that if we were too busy to get a dog and walk it, we were too busy full stop. So we got one. And she's been a great source of fitness and stress-busting for all our family.

There are other benefits to exercise too, apart from the health-related ones. For the busy Christian, going to the gym can be a real exercise (pardon the pun) in multi-tasking. Watching the TV screens at the gym is a chance to catch up on the news. While I'm tramping up and down on the wretched machines I get my one chance of the week to watch daytime TV, to find out what the latest music video looks like or listen to a radio station I wouldn't normally tune in to. For your information, in case you haven't been paying attention to these things, the radio station in question is dreadful, daytime TV is mind-numbingly tedious and the latest music video is hard to tell apart from a soft-porn film. But at least I am aware of what is going on in popular culture.

On a deeper level, I have valued very much the encounters I've had with people before my aerobics class, or around the water-cooler. It's one of the places (along with the school gate) that I can meet people. For busy Christians whose every waking hour is taken up with work, family and church-focused activities, the gym, the golf course and the aerobics studio are places where you can meet – wait for it – *people who aren't Christians!* Yes, really. As one of my friends once said, 'I have a real heart for the lost. I just don't know any.' The places where people exercise are the places where all of humanity mixes (well, the fit ones anyway) and it's good for Christians to be there, being themselves, talking about what makes them tick, sharing their faith (when they get their breath back enough to talk, that is).

There is something very therapeutic about doing exercise. Apart from the fairly obvious things like stopping you from having a heart attack or dying early of stress-related illness, it's a fairly unproductive activity. What is 'gained' by walking the dog, or running around the block, or stamping up and down on a step machine? Nothing in terms of work done or mortgage paid or meals cooked. That's why it's good to do it sometimes, to release ourselves from the obsession with always being productive, getting things done, achieving. I spend a lot of my life running around, to the shops, to school, to church, to the latest training event. So I like the fact that when I'm on the treadmill at the gym I don't actually go anywhere; when I'm on the step machine, I don't climb anywhere; when I'm on the rowing machine I don't actually move. Call me sad and warped, but I quite like that.

Of course you're too busy to build regular times of exercise into your routine. We all are. It's just that unless you put it in *first*, unless you count it, like eating and sleeping, as one of the basic building blocks of human existence, which need to go in there before anything else, you'll never fit it in. I can honestly say that since I started building exercise into my weekly routine I have felt far more energetic and healthier than ever before, and therefore more able to cope with the stresses and strains that busyness brings.

Fashion

Not only is it the case that 'we are what we eat'; we also 'feel how we look', we're told. One of the most popular television programmes dealing with fashion and image is *What Not to Wear*. The presenters take on a sartorially challenged person and help him or her to dress in a way that suits their shape and lifestyle, or as the BBC publicity expresses it, they 'take style-challenged individuals on a journey towards tailored self-esteem'. The programme doesn't deal with clothes alone. It deals with emotions and self-worth. It specifically targets people who have been through a major life disturbance of some sort – widows and widowers, women who had undergone a mastectomy, teenage mums – and sorts their wardrobe out with the aim of sorting their lives out. One episode recently featured the case of a middle-aged woman who wanted to improve her relationship with her daughter. How should she achieve this? By taking the advice of the presenters and paying a bit more attention to her appearance. Then her daughter would feel better about her mother and her daughter's life would improve as a result. A rival programme, *Trinny and Susannah Undress*, is likewise a slightly bizarre mix of style advice and relationship counselling. The message coming at us loud and clear is that if you improve the way you look, you will feel better as a result. Looks are everything. Fashion is king.

There is some truth in the idea that feeling happy about your appearance leads you to feel better generally. There is no point pretending that our souls are totally divorced from our bodies. Feelings are affected by appearance, and it is not wrong to want to dress well, but we have to ask some questions about underlying motivation. Are we taking on board the message that we are not worth much if we don't wear the latest trends and look eternally youthful? Do we value ourselves for who we are and for whom God has made us to be, no matter what we're wearing at the moment?

Most references in the Bible about clothes are about taking them off or tearing them in repentance! Jesus again puts fashion in perspective: 'And why do you worry about clothing? Consider the lilies of the field, how they grow; they neither toil nor spin, yet I tell you, even Solomon in all his glory was not clothed like one of these' (Mt. 6.28–29). Despite his words, clothes are not unimportant in the life and ministry of Jesus.

When Jesus is transfigured, his clothes become shiny too: 'And while he was praying, the appearance of his face changed, and his clothes became dazzling white' (Lk. 9.29). Now there's a makeover and a half. You can't get that in Boden.

Clothing is part of what is offered to the poor and needy as a sign of love and acceptance: 'whatever you do for the least of one of these you do for me'. The descriptions of the end of time from the book of Revelation include vivid depictions of what God's people will be wearing as well as what they will be doing and saying: 'Around the throne are twenty-four thrones, and seated on the thrones are twenty-four elders, dressed in white robes, with golden crowns on their heads' (Rev. 4.4). Clothes are not everything but they are not insignificant.

Clothes and jewellery have been in the news recently, as the banning of youths wearing hoodies from shopping centres, the dismissal of a Muslim teaching assistant who wore the veil to work and the rights or otherwise of a Christian airline employee to wear a cross around her neck have all hit the headlines. Clothes are much more than coverings for the body. They are symbols of identity and belonging.

Paul in his letter talks about the need for Christians to *show* who they are and their distinctiveness from the world around them by what they wear, as well as by what they do and say. To the Christian women of the day, many of whom lived in a culture where wearing jewellery was a sign of prostitution, he says: 'Women should dress themselves modestly and decently in suitable clothing, not with their hair braided, or with gold, pearls, or expensive clothes' (1 Tim. 2.9). Peter writes: 'Do not adorn yourselves outwardly by braiding your hair, and by wearing gold ornaments or fine clothing, rather, let your adornment be the inner self with the lasting beauty of a gentle and quiet spirit, which is very precious in God's sight' (1 Pet. 3.3). Mmmm. I'm not sure about the gentle and quiet spirit bit. I would want to argue that it's entirely possible to be 'feisty and loud' and still have real inner beauty as a woman. But the point still stands that image is about what we wear, yes, but it's also about who we are inside.

How much time do you spend on clothing and image – shopping, choosing, wearing, worrying? Is it a source of outer busyness and inner stress for you? Or do you have a healthy, godly perspective on your wardrobe? We are 'made in the image of God', both male and female. 'What not to wear' is all very well, but perhaps someone needs to formulate a programme to counter the obsession with clothing and outward appearances, called 'How Not to Be'!

House and home

As a society we are growing more and more suspicious of the big bad world outside our front doors where lurk drug users, homeless people, terrorists, predatory paedophiles and dragons. So we stay in, shut our front doors (replete with attractive brass-effect door furniture) and decorate our living-rooms in a tasteful shade of duck-egg blue. The Englishman's home truly has become his castle.

We love our homes, but we can't really afford them. House prices in most parts of the UK are now so high that the average person needs to work like stink in order to pay for the privilege of owning a home at all. We worship our homes, but we don't really have the time to run them. I saw an advert recently in a magazine for home management services, a grander version of a house-keeper, who would not only iron your clothes, but organize your life for you too. As with exercise, sleep, food and fashion, we have an uneasy relationship with houses. We want them to be nice, but we're too busy to do much about it. Is 'home' a blessing or a millstone around your neck?

I have an ambivalent relationship with the whole house thing. On the one hand I really enjoy looking after a home and making it nice. It's the creative side of me that loves painting and decorating and designing nice things. I even like housework. I am a very sad, warped individual, I know, but I like hoovering. It's a control thing, I think. There's something about imposing a kind of order on my carpets that is quite impossible to achieve in other aspects of my life. And if I can't fully sort out my busyness, at least I can keep my toilet clean.

However, we do not own our own home. One of the side-effects of being clergy is that you get a house provided for you. This is great, unless it also means (as it does for many of my clergy friends) that you failed to buy a house for yourself when the property market was remotely affordable on the meagre stipend we earn. We don't own any property. As things stand at the moment we don't stand much chance of being able to own any (unless this book sells really well!). In some senses I feel somewhat liberated by not owning a home. There is no responsibility and if the boiler goes wrong I phone up the housing officer in the diocese and a man comes and fixes it for me and I don't have to pay him. On the other hand there is a great deal of security in owning your own home and the fact that we don't have one gives us the wobbles sometimes. Where will we live when we retire and the house isn't provided any more? Don't worry, we'll be fine in our cardboard box on the side of the M5.

Owning a home is often the very root cause of why people are so busy. The working father says, 'I need to stay longer at work because I need a promotion in order to pay the mortgage.' An expectant mother says, 'I can't afford to stop work when my baby is born because we'd never afford our mortgage.' Add to that the pressure of getting a home in the 'right' area of the country or in the catchment area of the 'right' school, and you have a recipe for huge headaches.

Is home a place of retreat from the hectic world, a secure and tranquil place in which really to be yourself? Or is it yet another source of stress which needs to be cleaned, maintained, updated and paid for, therefore adding to the stress? Let's take a look at what living in a house involves.

On being a domestic goddess

Allow me a moment of indulgence. I was amused to come across a little book published in 1949 called *The Housewife's Contact with Jesus*. This priceless little book offers uplifting Scripture verses and some words of spiritual inspiration to the busy housewife as she goes about her daily tasks. There are headings such as 'brushing your hair', 'dusting and cleaning', 'laying the table', 'making clothes' and 'mending boots' (something I do every day – don't you?). There's a helpful little Scripture verse for each one and some inspirational words to help you in your task. Next time you're in the supermarket, be encouraged: 'Shopping is always a problem. But as of old as today, Jesus himself knows all the answers to your shopping problems. It may be that he has set you the problem to prove you, and is waiting for you to consult him.' Or some words of wisdom when dealing with your servants: 'Here is another lovely example of Jesus that you can follow, by making friends with your servant. You will find that two friends can do far more than a mistress and a servant.' That's so true, don't you find? OK, so you might not need to make friends with your servant, in Jesus's name, but how do you invite God into all that 'home' entails for you?

There is a part of me that really baulks at the word 'home-maker'. As if to care for a house and home is a job or title, rather than a normal, everyday part of life. All men and women, whether they stay at home or go out to work, if they live in a house, are homemakers. I much prefer the title 'domestic goddess'. Nigella Lawson certainly started something when she published a cookbook with the sardonic title *How to be a Domestic Goddess*.[16] At the height of the feminist movement in the 1960s and 1970s, to call someone a 'domestic goddess' would have been to offer a vile insult. Today it is perfectly acceptable and in fact a high accolade to call someone a domestic goddess, but only dryly, with your tongue firmly planted in your cheek. What women today are saying is 'Hey, we can look sexy, wear frilly aprons and bake divine cakes, but only because we want to, not because we are under any male-imposed, oppressive compulsion to do so. We are at the kitchen sink because it's a good place to hang out, not because we're chained to it.'

As a recent interview with the designer Cath Kidston, whose floral fabrics and enamel kitchenware epitomize the rediscovery of all things homely and domestic, puts it: 'Her things are all about playing at being a domestic Goddess – because life is too short and too full of exciting distractions to be one for real.'[17] Nigella too (bless her) says in the introduction to *How to be a Domestic Goddess*: 'So what I'm talking about is not being a domestic goddess exactly, but feeling like one.'[18] The initiative is ours. It's about how we feel inside rather than what we do outside. And so we enjoy home-making, but we don't *have* to do it.

A godly perspective

Do you see your home as a sacred place? We have grown up with a Christianity that finds it hard to value the physical – both our bodies and the places we put them in. We have been very good at doing the 'spiritual' bit outside the home, for instance in church, but often we haven't learnt to relate to the sacred in our own

16. Nigella Lawson, *How to be a Domestic Goddess* (Chatto and Windus, 2000).
17. Sarah Vine interview with Cath Kidston, *The Times*, 8 April 2006.
18. Lawson, *How to be a Domestic Goddess*, p. vii.

homes – the place where we spend a lot of our time. Building a good place to live (in every way) is not only a physical but also a spiritual activity, and one worth spending time on. There is something inherently godly about caring for the space in which you live and those who live in it with you.

In the Bible, the home was an important, hallowed place. In the Old Testament, house and the home were blessed with the peace of God. Abraham provides the model for a race where family, home and descendants are gifts of God. Houses were the central focus of living and being to the Jewish people, so their exile in the wilderness recorded in Exodus must have been excruciating. The theme of the 'house of God' was central for them too, and led to their building the ark of the covenant.

So important are homes that the Psalmist tells us God himself is called 'our dwelling place', our home. Jesus describes the way God relates to his followers as his being 'at home' with them: 'Those who love me will keep my word, and my Father will love them, and we will come to them and make our home with them' (Jn 14.23). Much of Jesus's ministry was carried on in homes, as in the Mary and Martha story. The conversion of Zaccheus in Luke Chapter 19 takes place in his home (as the song goes, 'I'm coming to your house for tea!'). The lame man is lowered through the roof of someone's home for Jesus to heal him. In the house of Simon the Pharisee (in Luke 7), a woman pours ointment over Jesus's feet and her sins are forgiven. In Jesus's ministry, the home was a place of healing, conversion, redemption and forgiveness. Most significantly of all, the last supper – the institution of our holy communion – took place in the upper room of an ordinary house.

The early Church met not in synagogues or temples, but in homes. The spiritual and the domestic were inseparable in the natural sacredness of home life. The metaphor Jesus uses to speak of our life in eternity is one of homecoming: 'In my Father's house there are many dwelling-places. If it were not so, would I have told you that I go to prepare a place for you? And if I go and prepare a place for you, I will come again and will take you to myself, so that where I am, there you may be also' (Jn 14.2–3). We talk about heaven as our 'eternal home', a metaphor richly evocative of a sense of comfort, peace and security. Our earthly homes can never be perfect (mine isn't anyway – too much dust), but we can see them as a foretaste of heavenly comfort and peace.

In a culture where to own one's own home is the ultimate ambition, what does this say about our attitude to what we possess and where we live? Perhaps the temptation is to see the bricks we own as our security, adding to the stress as we endeavour to keep up with maintaining this source of protection. Is our ultimate trust in the God who is our 'dwelling place' or in the house we pay a mortgage on?

Now there's no need to get too pious about it. Sound financial decision-making leads most people to recognize that for many reasons owning a home is a good idea. But we are constantly challenged by Jesus's nomadic, homeless existence: 'Foxes have holes, and birds of the air have nests; but the Son of Man has nowhere to lay his head' (Mt. 8.20). The ultimate reward, he says, is reserved for those who hold lightly to the things of earth in favour of the things of eternity:

> Peter began to say to him, 'Look, we have left everything and followed you.' Jesus said, 'Truly I tell you, there is no one who has left house or brothers or sisters or mother or father or children or fields, for my sake and for the sake of the good news, who will not receive a hundredfold now in this age – houses, brothers and sisters, mothers and children, and fields, with persecutions – and in the age to come eternal life'. (Mk 10.28–30).

It is hard teaching indeed. Our security is not to be in bricks and mortar, but in the God who provides them.

Partnership and sacrifice

How might men and women support each other better in this area of rest, relaxation, body and home? The quest for health and wholeness is something that is common to all and supporting one's brother or sister in how they spend their time off, how they see their bodies and what they do with their homes is a godly calling.

In Mt. 5.9, Jesus says, 'Blessed are the peacemakers, for they will be called children of God.' Jesus isn't simply referring to peace as being the absence of war and conflict, but to the concept of shalom – that kind of total well-being that is the presence of all the fullness of God in a person's life, a wholeness of body, mind and spirit. The peacemakers are therefore those who encourage and enable this kind of wholeness in the lives of their friends, family, community and world.

The biblical understanding of shalom is that it is not individual but communal:

> The Biblical concept of 'shalom' is about much more than just peace. It expresses an aspiration of well-being and wholeness that is not just for individuals, but for communities. It is about how people relate to each other and live interdependently and includes values such as sharing, mutuality, justice and freedom.[19]

So to support another person in their seeking after 'shalom' is to be commended.

In order for one person to find shalom, another person might have to make sacrifices. It is simple economics. On a very basic level and using some very simple examples, if I persuade my husband to stay in bed for a much-needed extra hour's sleep on a Saturday morning while I get up to take the dog out, I am encouraging shalom in his life. If I sacrifice some of the time in my day when I could be sitting with my feet up, to making a cake that I know my daughter will love, I'm bringing shalom into her life. If my friend is really busy at work but puts aside the time to meet me for a long lunch, she is encouraging shalom for me. If I spend a little more on a product that enables a farmer in the developing world to make a fair living, that is shalom. Shalom is about community as well as close relationships.

The point is, though, that the welfare of body, mind and spirit is

19. Introduction on the homepage of The Shaftesbury Society, www.shaftesburysoc.org.uk.

something we need to attend to, but also something we need to help and support others in. It's much easier to have a balanced, healthy attitude to your time, your body and your home when others are supporting you in the venture of healthy living.

In Lk. 13.10–17, Jesus heals a woman who was bent over and crippled. For that woman, such a disability and its associated cultural stigma would have meant she was unable to find wholeness in many areas, financial, social, emotional. Jesus healed her and set her free. The trouble was he did it on the Sabbath, much to the consternation of the synagogue officials. Jesus refuses to countenance their religiosity and concern with rules above people and gives it to them straight: 'You hypocrites! Does not each of you on the Sabbath untie his ox or his donkey from the manger, and lead it away to give it water? And ought not this woman, a daughter of Abraham whom Satan bound for eighteen long years, be set free from this bondage on the Sabbath day?' When he said this, all his opponents were put to shame; and the entire crowd was rejoicing at all the wonderful things that he was doing (Lk. 13.15–17).

If we are likewise to live by Sabbath principles, we will be people who set others free to find wholeness and shalom, as they do also for us. This 'setting free' might also mean that we avoid doing anything that damages or binds the material, bodily or spiritual well-being of others. As Marva J. Dawn puts it: 'Sabbath keeping exposes our political illusions. To think about God and the lifestyle to which he calls us forces us to see that our political power plays do not accomplish God's purposes.'[20] She is talking particularly about the politics of war, but her words could quite easily apply to the politics of gender. In gender terms, shalom may well mean respecting and valuing the other sex, and not reinforcing negative stereotypes about each other, particularly in reference to the concept of body and image.

Some of the preoccupation of (especially young) women with body image and fashion is driven by a perceived pressure on them to act and look like pornographic representations of stereotypical male fantasies. In a piece in *Good Housekeeping* magazine, Decca Aitkenhead discusses the growing trend amongst young women

20. Marva J. Dawn, *Keeping the Sabbath Wholly* (Eerdmans, 1989).

for dressing and behaving in a highly sexualized way which, they claim, is simply being 'liberated'. She says:

> My problem is that I have great difficulty believing that women's sexual liberation would look so much like every teenage boy's wet dream. Modern young women – whether it's club reps on *Ibiza Uncovered*, *Big Brother* contestants, men's mag *High Street Honeys* . . . are all modelling themselves on an old-fashioned, fundamentally pornographic idea of man's ideal woman.'[21]

A man who respects and cherishes women, who never lets himself collude with this form of oppression and encourages others in his society to emulate his example, is a man bringing the values of shalom to his society and culture. Similarly a woman respects a man if she does not allow herself to collude with superficial images of men as weak and helpless around the home, as hopeless sexual predators on the streets and as obsessed only with football and beer.

There is a form of *gender* hospitality which says that, just as we invite people into our homes, we can also invite people into our worlds, especially our worlds of leisure and rest, with respect and honour, getting to know them for who they are, rather than for who we have heard they might be.

Stepping above

God is concerned with the practical as well as the eternal. He is interested in the whole of our lives – mind, spirit and body. It may be that one of the areas addressed in this chapter is a source of stress for you. The Bible speaks of redemption in Christ as affecting much more than just our souls and spirits. Just as sin had spiritual and physical effects on humanity, so Christ's redeeming work encompasses the bodily as well as the spiritual.

21. Decca Aitkenhead, 'We burnt our bras for this?', *Good Housekeeping*, December 2006.

We are doing a redemptive thing to attend to the well-being of our bodies and our homes, and to help others to find this kind of shalom too. What might redemption in this area mean for you? It might mean taking the time you need to rest, to do what fires you, to devote time to your holistic well-being, to have fun, to do more exercise, to enjoy being a domestic goddess (or god).

Ask yourself some questions and reflect prayerfully on the answers: How well do I rest? What is my pattern of Sabbath? What helps me to relax? Do I allow myself enough time and space in my day to do some of those things? What makes me tick? How do I view my body? How might I see my home as a place of security, but also as a place of hospitality? How might I bring more shalom into my life and the lives of those around me?

And relax . . .

Having hope

10

Making choices for the hard times

It's fine when life is going swimmingly. You can go to work, get involved in church, take exercise, spend time with your friends and family, cook nice meals, decorate your home and pray. When you have the energy and the resources to live life to the full, you go for it. What happens, though, when the wheels drop off, when your life falls to bits, when things go wrong, when you get ill, when you experience loss, when you are left with neither the energy nor the resources to get up in the morning, let alone get out there and 'have it all'?

The main hypothesis of this book has been that there is nothing wrong with being busy. Busyness can be good, fulfilling and joyful when it is manageable and when it is the right kind of busyness. But when busyness goes wrong, that is when the problems occur – when busyness becomes over-busyness, when exciting pressure becomes draining stress, when fulfilling opportunities become frightening anxieties, when vocation becomes obligation.

Road-safety adverts have taught us that a car crash at 20 miles an hour is nasty, but is less likely to cause significant harm than a car crash at 80 miles an hour. That's when significant damage to yourself or others is likely to occur. So it is with busyness. If things go wrong in a manic, over-busy life, the damage is likely to be substantially greater than if things go wrong at a steady pace.

It is a well-known fact that stress can lead to significant illness. It also comes out of the blue to people who are not particularly stressed and busy. For busy people, though, the pain of having to slow down or stop can be the worst aspect of illness.

What happens when being busy is making you ill? And what happens to our relationships when things go belly up? Even the most solid, mutual, supportive relationships struggle when life gets really tough.

I know this from experience.

Messages: When your world falls apart

Three years ago, on a September morning, I was eating my breakfast when I began to choke. I got up from the table to spit my mouthful of tea into the sink when suddenly a feeling of numbness began in my mouth, spread down my right arm and into my leg. By the time I had stumbled to the nearest chair I was completely paralysed down one side, my mouth was lopsided and droopy, I couldn't speak properly and I began to lose consciousness. I knew the symptoms of stroke and was convinced I was having one. I was 33, the fit, healthy mother of two young children and here I was having a stroke, so I thought. I thought I was probably going to die. Fortunately Mat was at home and rang for an ambulance. The paramedic arrived and confirmed that he suspected a stroke too, but said this was extremely rare in such a young person. I was rushed to the nearest accident and emergency department where, thankfully, over the next few hours, the feeling began to return to my arm and leg and my speech came back. I was over the worst, apparently.

I was sent home shaken, shocked and with an appointment to see a neurologist. Several months followed where I was very unwell. I had no occurrence of the dramatic events of that day, but I did have several alarming episodes of dizziness, pins and needles and pain in my chest and my head. I had every test it is possible to have, including MRI brain scans. (I still have the films from those scans in an envelope in my study. It's strangely reassuring to have pictures of my own brain!)

The tests could find nothing physically wrong and slowly but surely I began to feel better. Today I am left with no ill effects from what happened and it is still a mystery. In a way I am grateful for the lack of diagnosis – I didn't have cancer or a stroke or a heart problem or multiple sclerosis or any of the other alarming and frightening diseases that I had managed to find on the Internet that fitted my symptoms. But it left me with many unanswered questions. If there was nothing physically wrong with me, what had caused the dramatic collapse that morning?

In the months that followed, several people spoke of stress and anxiety as a possible cause for what had happened. I know I was a busy person, but could stress alone really have caused such an alarming episode? Above all I was left (and this still hasn't gone away completely) with a vague fear that any moment might be my last. Despite much prayer and ministry about the whole event I still worry that there might be something wrong that I'm not aware of. It has given me a respect for the fragility of life and an increased consciousness of the presence of God through it all.

Since the 'Bad Thing' (I don't really know what else to call it) happened to me I have spoken to several people who have had similar, unexplained but alarming physical problems and who have also been told that it may be something to do with their busy lifestyles. Can stress *really* have this much of an effect, or are people simply trying to help their friends slow down by attributing their symptoms to their hectic ways?

Commonly cited physical symptoms of stress include headaches, migraines, insomnia, back and neck aches, nausea, twitching, appetite changes and sweating. The long-term effects of stress can include heart disease, high blood pressure, arthritis, gastrointestinal problems and even cancer. However, being aware that stress can do this doesn't always help when you're in the middle of it. When I was ill, every time someone told me my symptoms were probably caused by stress, I found myself feeling guilty for being stressed and trying very, very hard not to be so stressed, which made me feel . . . stressed. It's one thing to know that you might need to slow down a bit, but it can get incredibly irritating when people around you attribute every ache and pain to being too busy.

I have a friend who is well known as someone who works just a little bit too hard. One day he went out for a dodgy seafood dinner, fainted in the bathroom that night and knocked himself out on the sink. He got very annoyed with the number of people who came up to him over the following days, peered into his bruised and battered face with a look of concern (you know the one – head slightly to one side, hand on the shoulder) and said to him, 'You know, you really must slow down'. 'What has some dodgy sushi got to do with the fullness of my diary?', he wanted to scream. Knowing that your busyness can make you ill is one thing. Knowing what to do about it is a whole different matter.

So whether or not my Bad Thing was caused by my busyness (and I still very much doubt it was the only cause), I did learn some important lessons about perspective, pace and people, as follows.

. . . that I'm really glad to be alive

When you have been in a place where you honestly believe (rightly or wrongly) that you might die, and you don't, every moment afterwards becomes a gift and a blessing. As Bill Hybels says: 'When we come face to face with devastation we start to see life through stark new lenses.'[1] The 'new lenses' my Bad Thing gave me were an increased sense that life is delicate and fragile and must not be taken for granted. In the midst of the busyness and the rush it is necessary to savour each moment, because you don't know how many more moments you might have. Living life to the full might simply mean living each day as if it were the first day of the rest of your life – which of course, it is.

. . . that relationships are the most important thing

Toby was in the next-door room when the Bad Thing happened. He was watching the early morning edition of the children's TV programme *Tellytubbies* at the time. He was (mercifully) oblivious to

1. Bill Hybels, *Finding God in the Storms of Life* (IVP, 2002).

what was going on and didn't even take his eyes off the screen when I was carried out in a stretcher. I do remember a slightly absurd moment when I realized I might live my last minutes on earth to the *Tellytubbies* theme music, which seemed rather incongruous. But then, I also gave birth to the sound of Eminem singing 'Call Me Slim', as that was the ironic operating music of choice of the surgeon who performed my Caesarean. My life is punctuated with inappropriate soundtracks. I'm sure I'll get to heaven and the heavenly host will be singing the theme tune to *Antiques Roadshow* or something. What was I saying? Oh yes, relationships. It struck me as my son sat in the next-door room as I suffered this catastrophic collapse how much I didn't want to leave him. When you are faced with the possibility that you might not have an ongoing relationship with the people you hold most dear, it really makes you appreciate them.

In the midst of the busyness, the thing that matters most is your family and your friends. If busyness is getting in the way of those relationships, changes need to be made. It's oft quoted but it's true that no one ever said on their deathbed, 'I wish I'd spent more time at the office'.

... *that community matters*

The support of the community at Lee Abbey was invaluable to me in the hours, days and weeks following the Bad Thing. Within minutes of it happening, Mat had phoned the reception desk and a couple of people came to pray with me while we were waiting for the ambulance. When I returned from hospital and as I recovered, I was quite overwhelmed by the prayers and practical support that were offered to me and my family.

The Body of Christ comes into its own when there is suffering in part of it. The Bishop of Bristol, Mike Hill, and his wife were involved recently in a horrific car crash, which left the bishop with a broken shoulder and his wife with severe spinal injuries. In the weeks following the accident their progress was reported via a weblog, which was for a while one of the top ten most visited weblogs in the country. One posting read:

This blog has been visited almost 35,000 times since it was first posted. The family have received over 1,000 cards and separate emails. Though not all this support has come from Christians, which in itself is moving, the vast majority has, proving St Paul's teaching that when one part of the body hurts, the rest of the body feels it. All of this is indeed, 'love of another kind'.

There is something very special about the love of a Christian community for each other. Whilst we know that it is not all sweetness and light all the time, at 'times like these' the love of Christ comes to the fore. Sometimes it is in the suffering that the gift of community is most keenly felt. Henri Nouwen, who experienced great suffering first hand in the l'Arche community for severely handicapped people, says this:

> In community we say, 'Life is full of gains and losses, joys and sorrows, ups and downs – but we do not have to live it alone. We want to drink our cup together and thus celebrate the truth that the wounds of our individual lives, which seem intolerable when lived alone, become sources of healing when we live as part of a fellowship of mutual care.'[2]

. . . that the world carries on

One of the hardest things I found about the months I was ill was stopping. I had to learn to sit still and simply do nothing, as part of my recovery involved plenty of rest. A Christian doctor I know 'prescribed' for me times of breathing deeply and meditating on God as part of the road to health, along with sensible eating and exercise. I was surprised at how difficult I found this enforced cessation of activity. I am used to being someone always on the go.

2. Henri Nouwen, *Can You Drink the Cup?* (Ave Maria Press, 1996), quoted in John and Gay Perry, 'Community and Healing', in Ineson and Edmondson (eds), *Celebrating Community: God's gift for today's world*, p. 81.

I found 'being still' while the world around me carried on as normal very frustrating. I wanted to be joining in.

What made the whole thing so difficult was that the world didn't stop just because I had. The family home was cared for (mostly by Mat and my mother) but I didn't have much to do with it. My colleagues carried on with work, but without me. The world kept turning, even though I was in bed. There is something deeply humbling and not a little disconcerting about this. As busy people, we can often be tempted to feel that we are indispensable and that if we don't do it all the world around us would grind to a halt. It's not true.

When you are very busy, a sense of perspective doesn't go amiss. Nick Cuthbert gives this advice to church leaders: 'You will never survive leadership by believing it all hangs on you. Get your life into the perspective of heaven and of eternity. Realize that your part is essential to the whole but it is not *the* whole.'[3] For 'leadership' substitute 'life' and that applies to everyone. This isn't an easy lesson for busy-philes to learn. But it's an important one.

The Bible is good at giving a sense of perspective. The book of Ecclesiastes pours healthy scorn on the activity and busyness of humanity in the light of eternity: 'What does man gain from all his labour at which he toils under the sun? Generations come and generations go, but the earth remains forever' (Eccl. 1.3–4). Sometimes we can get so full of our own importance that our concerns can seem like the only ones on earth. The wisdom of Ecclesiastes reminds us that when we get preoccupied with the busyness, there is another way of looking. Being busy may feel to be one of the most significant aspects of many of our lives. It is also perhaps the least significant.

This came home sharply to me the other day, when I heard of a 39-year-old mother who has inoperable breast cancer. I had been having a stressful day where I was trying like mad to fit everything into my busy life. When I heard that news it put everything else into perspective. There I was worrying about how I would fit in doing all my jobs. There she was worrying about who might care

3. Nick Cuthbert, *How to Survive and Thrive as a Church Leader* (Monarch Books, 2006), p. 112.

for her child if she died. How fortunate I am only to have to worry about the jobs.

A godly perspective

One of the hardest things about the tough times is seeing God and God's purposes in the midst of it all. Some people manage it. Some people feel closer to God, know his love more keenly and find it easier to pray when life is hard. I admire those people but I have to say, I am not one of them. For me, God always seems more present and more real, more significant when things are going well, the sun is shining and everything's hunky-dory. I find it harder to know what God is up to when the dark clouds gather and it buckets down.

I suppose it is because I truly believe that God has to be all-powerful (otherwise he wouldn't be God) and he has to be loving (otherwise he wouldn't be good). So if he is completely loving and completely powerful why doesn't he act to make everything better? I know all the theology. I know about evil and the Fall and the causes of suffering in the world. I've done theology courses on 'The problem of evil' and Bible studies on 'Why does God allow suffering?'. I've read Moltmann's *The Crucified God* and C.S. Lewis's *The Problem of Pain*. But when you're in the middle of the hard times, it is often the more instinctive feelings, rather than the well-thought-out theology, that comes to the fore.

So I do find it hard to see God in the hard times. I'm just being honest. I don't have even a few of the answers, let alone all of them, but the following are a few thoughts that have been a comfort to me in the desert moments and that might help you.

God knows about suffering

People often ask me as a minister why God allows suffering. It's the hardest question to answer and I don't often try to. But one thing I do say is that whenever there is suffering, wherever people are wounded and hurting, God weeps too.

In the person of Jesus, God became the suffering servant: 'a man of sorrows and familiar with suffering' (Isa. 53.3). Dorothy L. Sayers wrote:

> For whatever reason God chose to make people as they are – limited and suffering and subject to sorrows and death – he had the honesty and courage to take his own medicine. Whatever game he is playing with his creation, he has kept his own rules and played fair. He can exact nothing from us that he has not exacted from himself. He has himself gone through the whole human experience, from the trivial irritations of family life and the cramping restrictions of hard work and lack of money to the worst horrors of pain and humiliation, defeat, despair, and death. When he was man, he played the man. He was born in poverty and died in disgrace and thought it all worthwhile.[4]

I have always found it very comforting that even after the Resurrection, when the power and majesty of God had been evidenced most fully and when Jesus had done what no other person had done – defeated death – he was still wounded. As he appears to the disciples, he invites them to 'put your finger here; see my hands. Reach out your hand and put it into my side' (Jn 20.27). Victorious, but wounded. For those of us who are type A personalities and identify more with the being victorious bit, it is good to remember that there is always woundedness too and that both are found in the nature and experience of God himself.

God cares

Archbishop William Temple wrote these moving lines: ' "There cannot be a God of love," people say, "because if there was, and he looked upon the world, his heart would break." The church points

4. Dorothy L. Sayers, *Greed or Chaos?* (Harcourt Brace, 1949), p. 4.

to the Cross and says, "It did break." ' The overriding quality of God is love. In the midst of suffering and pain, he continues to *be* love. And we are told that nothing will be able to separate us from the love of God in Christ Jesus: 'neither death nor life, neither angels nor demons, neither the present nor the future, nor any powers, neither height nor depth, nor anything else in all creation' (Rom. 8.38–39). Not even busyness.

Jesus's pre-eminent reaction to those who are stretched and harassed, whether by being over-busy or by any other kind of suffering, is to be understanding and compassionate. I think sometimes we feel that if we allow ourselves to 'bring suffering on ourselves' by becoming stressed and over-busy, Jesus looks down on us with annoyance, angry that we've allowed ourselves to get ourselves into this mess when we really should be still and peaceful and trusting. Quite the opposite. Jesus is understanding and gentle: 'When he saw the crowds, he had compassion on them, because they were harassed and helpless, like sheep without a shepherd' (Mt. 9.36).

Consider how he viewed the rich young man looking for validation for his accumulation of wealth: 'Jesus looked at him and loved him' (Mk 10.21). Remember his tender rebuke: 'Martha, Martha . . . you are worried and upset about many things.' Jesus's response to everyone he met was to love them *in their present circumstances* – and to draw them gently into new ways of living.

Jesus does offer rest and refreshment, but in the middle of life and hardship, rather than as an alternative to it:

Come to me, all you who are weary and burdened, and I will give you rest. Take my yoke upon you and learn from me, for I am gentle and humble in heart, and you will find rest for your souls. For my yoke is easy and my burden is light. (Mt. 11.28–30)

Being busy doesn't mean you will necessarily be weary and burdened. But if you are, Jesus promises rest. But it is rest for our souls – maybe even in the midst of busyness.

Even when life is hard, God is still God

My favourite book of the Bible is the book of Job. The theology of the book of Job can be summarized like this (and you'll have to excuse the language): 'Shit happens but God is God.' I find that somehow very comforting, but as G.K. Chesterton says: 'It is the lesson of the whole work that man is most comforted by paradoxes.'[5] 'Life is difficult' (as M. Scott Peck once said),[6] but God is God, even if we don't always understand what he's up to.

Job tells the story of a man who is good and God-fearing and yet loses everything – his wife, his family, his possessions, his health, his dignity. The awkward thing about the whole story is that it begins with God *allowing* the devil to test Job, which is problematic to explain theologically. The God of the book of Job is a robust God who is able to take the complaining, questioning and doubts of his subjects and respond, without anger, but with authority, integrity and compassion. There are some wonderful passages where God, far from reaching down the comforting arm and the heavenly box of tissues, pulls himself to his full height and answers Job's questioning by reasserting his divine majesty, power, creativity and omnipotence with examples from the world of nature and the life of the animal kingdom:

> Brace yourself like a man; I will question you, and you shall answer me. 'Where were you when I laid the earth's foundation? Tell me, if you understand. Who marked off its dimensions? Surely you know! Who stretched a measuring line across it? On what were its footings set, or who laid its cornerstone while the morning stars sang together and all the angels shouted for joy?' (Job 38.3–7)

The major point of the book of Job is that despite all the pain and suffering, despite all the questions, Job remains true to the God who knows his suffering and yet reasserts his supremacy and eternal nature.

---

5. 'Introduction to the Book of Job', in *Chesterton Day by Day: The wit and wisdom of G.K. Chesterton*, ed. Michael W. Perry (Inkling Books, 2002).
6. These are the opening words to M. Scott Peck, *The Road Less Travelled* (Arrow, 1990).

Job 'remonstrates with his Maker because he is proud of his Maker. He even speaks of the Almighty as his enemy, but he never doubts, at the back of his mind, that his enemy has some kind of a case which he does not understand'.[7] What the book of Job gives is a sense of perspective. Although suffering may be great, God is still God.

Partnership and sacrifice

The marriage service contains the vow that husband and wife will take each other 'for better, for worse, for richer, for poorer, in sickness and in health'. It is a promise more easily said than done.

What happens to friendships and close relationships when life is hard? How do we 'hold the Christ light' for each other in the darkness? What happens when both are in the dark and no one can find the matches?

What I haven't told you about the time when the Bad Thing happened is that it couldn't have come at a worse time for Mat. His mother had been suffering from cancer for some years and in the days before my collapse, her condition had deteriorated. At about the same time as I was ill and having brain scans (we were still in the 'it might be a brain tumour' days), it became clear that she was dying. Mat was faced with a heart breaking choice – to stay with his sick wife, not yet knowing what or how serious my illness was, or to go and be with his dying mother, who was in hospital hundreds of miles away. He did go and spend some time with his mother, but not as much as he would have liked to have done if all had been well at home.

In those days when I was ill and he was grieving, we found it very difficult to support each other. Part of the frustration came in knowing that, normally, if Mat was going through a hard time, I would be there to support him and vice versa. Each of us knew the other needed our help and care, but was unable to give it fully because of what was going on for us as individuals, as well as a couple.

7. Chesterton, 'Introduction to the Book of Job'.

When relationships are equal and pain comes in equal amounts for both partners, it is very difficult to lift your head above the fog enough to care for the other person. When you're used to leaning on each other, and neither of you is able to offer support, the result is that you both fall over.

The conclusion we came to is that the only one strong and consistent enough to lean on fully is God. This verse from Proverbs became particularly poignant: 'Trust in the Lord with all your heart and lean not on your own understanding' (Prov. 3.5).

What is needed is the ability to communicate clearly and effectively, even if you don't feel like it. Decide on principles in the good times that will still hold true in the hard times.

We had a very difficult few months, but with the help and support of some good friends and family, and as my illness cleared up, the fog began to lift and we were able to stand and support each other again. The experience has taught me that partnership between men and women, whether in marriage or in other kinds of relationships, is nothing if it cannot weather the storms as well as the sunny periods. And the only way it will do that is to have God as the central 'strut' of any relationship, for 'A cord of three strands is not quickly broken' (Eccl. 4.12).

The key to any relationship being able to weather the storms is being able to adapt to shifting circumstances, not all of them good, and learning to support and communicate in the chaos. In a scientific context, the word 'chaos' has a slightly different meaning from how it is generally understood as 'a state of confusion' or 'lacking any order'. Chaos, in scientific chaos theory, refers to 'an apparent lack of order in a system that nevertheless obeys particular laws or rules ... Although chaos is often thought to refer to randomness and lack of order, it is more accurate to think of it as an *apparent* randomness that results from complex systems and interactions among systems.' Anne Borrowdale suggests that chaos theory is a useful concept in describing how families and relationships can best learn to develop and adapt, in spite of challenging circumstances: 'flexibility in ways of managing life and family form allow us to respond to changes more creatively.'[8]

8. Anne Borrowdale, *Reconstructing Family Values* (SPCK, 1994), p. 19.

This applies to all relationships, not just in marriage and not just between individual men and individual women. Being able to live with a healthy sense of chaos allows any community to hold within it differences and disagreements, without everything always having to be nice and agreeable. The challenge to the Church of England at the moment, as it considers the consecration of women as bishops, is to learn to stand together as men and women, those who are for and those who are against, in the chaos, and live together well with the differences.

Stepping above

In all of the other sections of this book I have encouraged you to take time out to 'step above' the issue; to stand above the busyness and the chaos and make some informed choices about how you are going to live your life. Doing this is fairly straightforward when life is going well. What about when it all goes wrong?

With hardship and suffering, it is very difficult to step above and choose carefully to the same degree. 'I can see clearly now the rain is gone', goes the song, but what about when it's still wazzing it down? When 'all obstacles in my way' simply function as trip-hazards? Stepping above the pandemonium is tricky when you're in the middle of it. It's too much like lifting yourself up by your own bootlaces.

However, *being lifted above* by someone else might be a possibility. That someone else could be God: 'I waited patiently for the Lord; he turned to me and heard my cry. He lifted me out of the slimy pit, out of the mud and mire; he set my feet on a rock and gave me a firm place to stand' (Ps. 40.1). When I pictured this passage I had always imagined God standing on the edge of the pit reaching down to outstretched arms to haul the person out of the mud. That is, until someone pointed out to me that God might be lifting the person out *from below*. God is not above our suffering, looking down on us, but is with us in it, in the pit. And he has the strength to lift us up out of it.

190

Asking for clearer vision and to be lifted up 'out of the slimy pit' goes for over-busyness as much as anything else. It is always worthwhile praying that God might help you to see clearly what you should be doing and what you shouldn't, where he is leading and where he is not.

When you are in the middle of a hard time, a perfectly good prayer is: 'Lord, lift me up and help me to see clearly. Help me to have your perspective on what is happening here.' In 2 Kgs. 6 we read the story of how the King of Aram has sent forces to capture Elisha and his servant:

> When the servant of the man of God got up and went out early the next morning, an army with horses and chariots had surrounded the city. 'Oh, my lord, what shall we do?' the servant asked. 'Don't be afraid,' the prophet answered. 'Those who are with us are more than those who are with them.' And Elisha prayed, 'O Lord, open his eyes so he may see.' Then the Lord opened the servant's eyes, and he looked and saw the hills full of horses and chariots of fire all around Elisha.

God allowed Elisha and his servant to see the unseen world that surrounded them, to see God's purposes in the chaos. God is especially present to those who are in danger or pain, but sometimes it is a matter of asking God to open our eyes that we might see him.

I recall as a chaplain at Lee Abbey praying one day with a woman who had multiple sclerosis. The disease meant she was limited in her ability to move, to speak and to hear and she expressed the fact that she often felt like an outsider, on the edge of everything. Her sense of exclusion from church worship had left her feeling that she couldn't get close to God either. 'Everyone else is crowding around Jesus,' she said, 'and I can't get close enough to him.' I asked her to close her eyes and picture that scene – people crowding around, and herself some way off. Then I asked her: 'Where is Jesus?' 'Oh!' she said with delight in her face, 'he's not in the middle of the crowd. He's standing with me at the edge.' In that prayer, God had opened her eyes to see him right next to her in her suffering. He too was excluded from the crowd.

He was with her.

'I have come that you may have life'

11

Don't ask what the world needs. Rather ask, what makes you come alive? Then go and do it! What the world needs is people who have come alive.

(Howard Thurman)

Life's splendour forever lies in wait about each one of us in all its fullness, but veiled from view, deep down, invisible, far off. It is there, though, not hostile, not reluctant, not deaf. If you summon it by the right word, by its right name, it will come.

(Franz Kafka)

I want to be thoroughly used up when I die, for the harder I work the more I live. I rejoice in life lived for its own sake. Life is no 'brief candle' to me. It is a sort of splendid torch which I have got hold of for the moment, and I want to make it burn as brightly as possible before handing it on to future generations.

(George Bernard Shaw)

Get busy living or get busy dying.

(Andy Dufresne in *The Shawshank Redemption*)

The glory of God is a human being fully alive.

(St Iranaeus of Lyon, third century)

I have come that they may have life, and have it to the full.

(Jesus Christ)

I sometimes wonder whether Christians are so preoccupied with *getting it right* that we forget that Jesus's intention was that life should be *good*. Has busyness got in the way of this ideal or is it possible to be busy and peaceful? What did Jesus *really* mean by life in all its fullness?

Messages

The messages that are aimed at busy people seem to gather around two extreme poles. At one pole we have the time-management gurus (mainly secular) who tell us simply to organize our time better and all will be well. It is possible to be busy and successful (in fact you need to be busy to be successful) but you have to work hard to make it all fit. It is possible to have it all and have it when you want it, but you must be ruthlessly efficient and make time work for you.

At the other pole are those (usually Christian) who tell us that if we are to have any hope of surviving, let alone thriving in life, we have to stop. Busyness is an evil our culture has invented to make us stressed and to keep us far from God. The answer, they say, is to resist busyness at all costs, to slow down, to say no and to seek the still places where God may be found.

There has to be a middle way. What I hope this book has done is to show that being busy is fine and is good and is godly, if it is an informed, thought-out, chosen busyness. A busy but good life can include healthily all the elements of work, rest, home, friends, family, prayer and leisure, if they are chosen wisely and in partnership with those living around you. Being busy is no more and no less than living the life God intends you to live – and God can be found in the busyness as well as in the stillness. The key to it all is being able to listen well to the messages that we hear and interpret them for ourselves, to sit thoughtfully above the maelstrom and make decisions about what will occupy my time and what will not. Refuse to bow to cultural messages but interpret them. Allow God to renew your mind to see what is good and what is not. Stand above the messages and assess them with God's voice constantly in your ear.

Two things are clear. The first is this: if life is to be busy, it is not possible to go it alone. The resources and support we offer each other as men and women, as husbands and wives, as partners and friends, as parents and children, as churches and communities are essential in maintaining health and wholeness in busy living

The second is this: it is not possible to have it all. Or at least, it is not possible to have it all at once. Life is just not like that. If we are to live well in the things that really matter, in our relationships and in the vocation to which God calls us, then sacrifices will have to be made. The way of sacrifice is the way of the Cross and the way to which all Christians are called, whether busy or not: 'Those who find their life will lose it, and those who lose their life for my sake will find it' (Mt. 10.39).

You have to make a choice.

Sacrifice and partnership

Sacrifice

In Jn 10.10, Jesus says, 'The thief comes only to steal and kill and destroy; I have come that they may have life, and have it to the full.'

Having life and having it to the full has been one of the central themes of this book and we will explore it still further in this chapter. But what else did Jesus say in this passage? To find the answer to that question, we have to look at the sections that come before it and after it. In Jn 10.7–11 we read:

> Therefore Jesus said again, 'I tell you the truth, I am the gate for the sheep. All who ever came before me were thieves and robbers, but the sheep did not listen to them. I am the gate; whoever enters through me will be saved. He will come in and go out, and find pasture. The thief comes only to steal and kill

and destroy; I have come that they may have life, and have it to
the full. I am the good shepherd. The good shepherd lays down
his life for the sheep.'

This text used to conjure up for me an image of a rural, English
idyll, with green fields, fluffy white sheep and a little picket fence
with a pretty gate in it. Somewhere in Sussex probably. That was
until someone explained to me what 'the gate for the sheep' really
meant. In biblical times, shepherds did not come home at night to
the security of the villages. Often they stayed out all night on the
hills where the sheep were gathered into makeshift sheepfolds. The
sheepfold might have had walls on three sides (perhaps improvised
from brushwood), but the fourth side was left open so the sheep
could come in and out during the day. There was no door. At
night, the shepherd himself would lie down in the opening, so no
sheep could get in or out, 'except over his body'.[1]

It's all about sacrifice and laying down one's life. The gate is the
one who lays down his life for the sheep, literally laying himself
across the gateway to the sheepfold in order to protect them and
give them life. That is what Jesus does.

There are times when we must lay ourselves down for others
too. It doesn't need to be in holy, spiritual ways. Laying down
getting promotion – so you can get home earlier to spend more
time with your children. Laying down earning a salary – so you
can devote yourself to voluntary work. Laying down having the
perfect house in the right area – so you don't have to work all the
hours God sends to pay the mortgage. Laying down watching a
few more hours' telly – so that you can go and play squash with
your friend. For everything we make a choice. We lay some things
down. And we take other things up.

Both are important. The Christian way is one of sacrifice and
crucifixion. It is also one of life and resurrection. There is a time
for fasting, but there is also a time for feasting. There is a time to
say 'no' and there is a time to say a big, hearty, resounding 'yes'. It
is the paradox that makes the Christian faith so interesting and so

1. William Barclay, *Daily Study Bible: The Gospel of John* (The Saint Andrew Press, 1955), p.
67.

exciting. But we need to make sure we are living fully in both, and understanding both, not just one at the expense of the other.

As I have been writing this book I have been asking myself: 'What have I sacrificed in my busy life?' A lot. I have laid down my life often – for my husband, for my children, for the people and communities to whom I have ministered. What have I missed out on? Very little. I don't have much money, I don't own my own home – and I don't get to watch much telly. Not bad. I have been very busy but have had it all, or as much as is God's intention for my life. I truly have had life in all its fullness.

Partnership

But I couldn't have done anything if it hadn't been in partnership. Partnership is not just about marriage. I firmly believe that a redeemed partnership between men and women at all levels of life and society is a sign of redemption and hope for our times. Nothing is possible without it. When men and women learn to partner each other properly, to support each other rather than compete, to release each other rather than restrict each other to stereotypes or prescribed roles, to understand each other rather than deride each other, then many areas of life will begin to function more effectively – the workplace, the marriage, the home, the church, the community, the society.

You are yourself in relation to other people, especially other people from the other sex. As men and women, we have a role to play in helping each other to find 'life in all its fullness'. In order to do so, we need to recognize who we are as individuals and together as male and female, helping each other to fulfil our vocations and find a sustainable and healthy lifestyle. Recent years have seen a growth in the confidence of women in many areas, although not all. The challenge for men is to accept and delight in this increased confidence without feeling threatened or defensive or wanting to reclaim what has traditionally been 'masculine'. The challenge for women is to grow in confidence alongside the men with whom God has placed them in partnership, not belittling men or oppressing them, but helping them to grow too.

Life in all its fullness means humanity in all its fullness. Humanity in its fullness is made in the image of God in God's fullness. And God in his fullness made male and female in his image. So life in all its fullness must involve aspects of maleness and femaleness in partnership in all areas.

Living life to the full

Let's look at the context of the life in all its fullness passage again. Picture again the sheepfold and the gate for the sheep – Jesus himself. His promise is that we might come in and go out *through* him and find pasture. The life in all its fullness that Jesus offers links the sheepfold and the pasture; it guarantees that the sheep can go in and out. Being able to *go in and out* was the Jewish way of speaking about goodness in life, living that was secure and peaceful. Thus the writer of Psalm 121 knows that 'The Lord will keep your going out and your coming in'. Life inside and life outside are held together and reconciled, as are security and freedom. It's both an image of security (in the sheep pen) and plenty (in the pasture), of retreat and of engagement.

In very real terms there is plenty in life that would kill and destroy that freedom for us, not thieves and robbers, but stress, over-busyness, stereotypical restrictions on gender, tiredness, materialism, house prices, media pressure, perfectionism. All of these are well known to those who love to be busy. Jesus does not suggest that the sheep should be shut up in a closed, over-protected, hermetically sealed, risk-free space. Their food is outside in the pasture. They are meant to be out there, living their lives, feeding and being nourished.

Our calling is to life in its fullness; to life in the security of the sheep pen (in times of retreat, times of stillness, times at home with family and friends, times of stopping, times of taking stock, times of withdrawal and rest, times stepping above), as well as life in the pasture out there (at work, at home, at church, being busy, living).

The Greek word for 'fullness' or 'abundance' here – *perissos* – has several meanings. One of those is 'excess, extraordinary in size or in beauty, excessively large or numerous'. It can also mean 'surplus, that which is extra, or left over'. It is used in four other passages in the New Testament: in Mt. 5.37 ('Let your word be "Yes, Yes" or "No, No"; anything more than this comes from the evil one', i.e. when one has said the essential, *anything more* creates confusion); in Mk 6.51 ('Then he got into the boat with them and the wind ceased. And they were utterly astounded', i.e. surprise *beyond all measure*); in Rom. 3.1 ('What advantage, then, has the Jew?', i.e. what *more* does the Jew have); and in 2 Cor. 9.1 ('Now it is not necessary for me to write to you about the ministry of the saints', i.e. it is *superfluous* for me to write to you about this).[2]

What Jesus expresses therefore 'by life in all it fullness' is an excess, an abundance, a superfluous, overflowing, unnecessary, overwhelming load of life. Shed loads of life. We may not be able to 'have it all', but in Christ we are certainly promised more than enough:

> Life in all its fullness is not about having it all. It is about learning not to be afraid. It is feeling connected to everything that is. It is compassion. It is knowing we are loved. It is saying: 'Yes' to the moment at hand. The Good News is that these things are available to us, whatever our situation.[3]

The encouragement to have life in all its fullness is therefore an encouragement to live life out there, doing and achieving in the world, but at the same time keeping ourselves firmly rooted in the person of Jesus and our relationship with him. It is he and he alone who can offer safety, security and peace. It is he alone who can prevent our busyness becoming over-busyness. It is he alone who offers life, who is himself, the way the truth and the life. As Paul says, it is only in Jesus that we can achieve anything or be content:

> I rejoice in the Lord greatly that now at last you have revived your concern for me; indeed, you were concerned for me, but

2. I am grateful to the insights of Philippe B. Kabongo-Mbaya in the interpretation of this passage.
3. Jo Ind, 'Life in all its fullness', on the Student Christian Movement website, www.movement.org.uk.

had no opportunity to show it. Not that I am referring to being in need; for I have learned to be content with whatever I have. I know what it is to have little, and I know what it is to have plenty. In any and all circumstances I have learned the secret of being well-fed and of going hungry, of having plenty and of being in need. I can do all things through him who strengthens me.' (Phil. 4.10–13)

Stepping above

The following are some final snippets of advice on how to be busy and enjoy it, some suggestions about how to find 'life in all its fullness' as well as 'the peace that passes all understanding'.

Live in the present

John Lennon once said: 'Life is something that happens to you while you are busy making other plans.' I know so many people who live like this: 'One day, I'll sort my life out', 'One day I'll find the right job', 'One day I'll spend more time with my children', 'One day . . .'. Some people spend so much time making plans, thinking about the future, knowing that there is a dream out there somewhere but not being able to find it, that life passes them by and they don't even notice.

Learning to practise the sacrament of the present moment is one of the keys to being busy and being peaceful. So much of our stress comes from worrying about how we will 'fit things in' in the future or regretting how badly we spent our time in the past, that we fail to enjoy the present and all the present moment holds. One of the things I have tried to do (not always successfully) is to live in the present. This does not mean that you have no regard for the past, or that you never plan for the future, but that you live life in the present moment, with a healthy awareness of past and future, but not an obsession with them.

199

I don't know where you are as you read this, or what your day has been like so far. But there you are. Right now. In the present, drinking your coffee, or reading this in the bath, or whatever it is you are doing. You will carry with you your past and all that it has held for you – the joys and the pains. And you have tucked away somewhere your hopes and fears for the future. But this is today. And there you are. And there God is – God who is acutely present with you in everything you do. '*This* is the day the Lord has made. We will rejoice and be glad in it' (Ps 118:24) We worship the God who calls himself 'I am'. So why is it that sometimes we find 'living in the present' not as easy to do as it is to say?

What happened yesterday goes some way towards explaining who we are today and we need to know the past for our present healing and hope. But we can't live in the past. We can't live in what we did yesterday. If you regret some of the decisions about how you spent your time in the past, there is no benefit to be found in dwelling there and regretting. Learn from your mistakes, but forgive yourself and others. Make a choice to move forward into a new way of living.

We need to make plans for the future and have a clear vision of where we are going. Part of surviving in the busyness is making choices for the future, as well as for the present, choices that will determine where and how your time is spent. But you can't live in the future either. If we spend every day hankering after what is to come, we will be constantly twitchy. It's so easy for 'thinking about the future' to turn into worry about it. We need a sure hope, but not anxiety; expectation, but not impatience. Tomorrow is exciting but it is not here yet, and there is nothing we can do by worrying to change what it will be. A Senegalese proverb says: 'If you wait for tomorrow, tomorrow comes. If you don't wait for tomorrow, tomorrow comes.' As Jesus pointed out, 'do not worry about tomorrow, for tomorrow will bring worries of its own. Today's trouble is enough for today' (Mt. 6.34).

I am a terrible worrier. The temptation for me is always to think about what comes next, whether that's the next hour or the next five years. Therefore I find doing mindless things, like cooking or walking the dog, to be very therapeutic. They anchor me in the present while giving my mind the opportunity to remember safely the past and pray about the future. Apparently, I have this in common with D.H. Lawrence: 'I got the blues thinking of the future, so I left off and made some marmalade. It's amazing how it cheers one up to shred oranges and scrub the floor.'

We live now. This moment is God's gift to us, as we nurture more and more the art of savouring the present with thankful hearts, and of seeing God's presence in everything and the everyday. Each moment of every day, *this* very moment, is a means of grace and a vehicle for God's love and power. The proclamation 'Behold, I am making all things new' (Rev. 21.5) is not just a future promise but a statement about the continual renewing work of God in each moment of our lives, if we are open to it. Every situation, every relationship, brings us closer to divine grace, if we are ready to receive it.

Our God is 'I am'. But he is also the God 'who was and is and is to come' (Rev. 1.8). Perhaps it's just me, but I always react badly to the statement that 'God does not change'. I know in a sense that's right, but I find the concept slightly boring. I know what it means, I suppose. God is always faithful, always true, always constant, always there, eternal. But everything that is interesting in life changes – seasons change, landscapes develop, children grow, trends evolve. Things that stay the same speak to me of fossilization. God's *nature* doesn't change, but God is dynamic, exciting and vibrant. God seeks to engage with each of us uniquely, and in a new way for the day at hand.

Our calling is to invite God into the busyness and the chaos *today*, not waiting until tomorrow, allowing him to fill the present moment with his exciting (and perhaps risky) love and power. We live in a culture that is losing touch with its history and is so uncertain about its prospects that the present is a very shaky place to stand. Christians – yes, even busy ones – are able to model something different – firmly rooted in the past and with real hope for the future, secure in God's here and now.

Decide on your attitude

All too often Christians seem to have an attitude of fear, of timidity, of self-doubt, of failure. I know there is a great deal about our own lives, about the Church and about humanity in general that could be a good sight better. But we can only start to change any of it from now. Today more than ever the Church and the world need people with a 'can do' attitude (rather than an 'Oh, I'm not sure' attitude), people who see the glass as half full rather than half empty.

One of the most encouraging things God promises is 'the renewal of your mind' (Rom. 12:2). That sounds good to me because the way I see my life is very much determined by the way I think and feel about all that goes on in me and around me. We all have different personalities and some people find it easier to be optimistic than others. For a start, some people do have a great deal more to be optimistic about than others. I wonder if I would be able to write these words if I were a single mother living on benefits in a high-rise block of flats in Scunthorpe rather than a comfortably off vicar's wife sitting in her nice study in middle-class Bristol. Nevertheless, the point still stands: when it comes to busyness and making choices about our lives, we do have the opportunity to be more or less positive about the whole thing, whatever lands on our plate. Perhaps the Monty Python group were on to something when they sang 'always look on the bright side of life' in the Crucifixion scene of *Life of Brian*.

I have always called myself a feminist, especially in response to the shocked look on some people's faces when we get talking about gender issues and they say to me with horror, 'You're not a *feminist* are you?' They use the same voice they might use if they were asking me whether I was a mass murderer. Yes, I am a feminist. And one of the best definitions of feminist comes from the novelist and journalist Rebecca West who said: 'I myself have never been able to find out precisely what feminism is: I only know that people call me a feminist whenever I express sentiments that differentiate me from a doormat.' In that vein, I am a feminist. However (and this is the point I'm getting slowly towards), one of the things that has always annoyed me most about the feminist movement is its victim mentality. Women must always be victims, because men are always oppressors. Neither of those things is true, as I hope we have discovered in the course of this book. But the legacy of being the victim is one many women (and some men) hold dear. It is possible to live always as a victim, fearful and defensive, or to think differently and be the one who makes choices, the one who gets out there and changes things, the one who is positive about life.

Jesus came to bring us life and freedom and sometimes we just need to start living as if it were true. Following Christ, if nothing else, brings liberty and confidence. As Ps. 119.45–46 says: 'I will walk about in freedom, for I have sought out your precepts. I will speak of your statutes before kings and will not be put to shame.' Perhaps for some of us what is required is a rediscovery of confidence to live as God calls us to live, as men and women with a future and a hope in Christ, knowing that 'I can do all things through Christ who strengthens me' (Phil. 4:13) Not some things. All things.

In Deuteronomy God lays his commandments before the Israelite people with these words:

> 'Now what I am commanding you today is not too difficult for you or beyond your reach. It is not up in heaven, so that you have to ask, "Who will ascend into heaven to get it and proclaim it to us so we may obey it?" Nor is it beyond the sea, so that you have to ask, "Who will cross the sea to get it and proclaim it to us so we may obey it?" No, the word is very near you; it is in your mouth and in your heart so you may obey it. ... This day I call heaven and earth as witnesses against you that I have set before you life and death, blessings and curses. Now choose life, so that you and your children may live.' (Dent. 30.11–16, NIV).

Choose life. The offer of life in all its fullness is there before us. But we have to choose it. So don't be afraid of being busy. Make the right choices and live them to the full.

This is not withstanding the fact that life can be hard sometimes. It is clear that 'choosing life' is a good deal easier when work is going well, your family is happy, your church is growing and your bank account is healthy. It is less easy when you are unemployed, overworked, ill or stressed. Yet even then I believe it is possible to be more or less peaceful, more or less hopeful. One of my 'slogans to live by' is that attributed to Julian of Norwich: 'All will be well and all will be well and all manner of things will be well.' Don't think Julian was some bleary-eyed mystic who would say that, wouldn't she? No, this is the same woman who, when her mule got stuck on a mountain road in a rainstorm, dismounted, shook her fist at the sky, and shouted, 'God! If this is how you treat your friends, it's no wonder you don't have many'.

As I said, you've got to laugh.

Find your calling and live it (and only it)

Christians at their worst are suspicious, protective, defensive and withdrawn from the world around them. Christians at their best are radical, confident, challenging, prophetic and engaged with the world around them. We are living in an age of unparalleled opportunity for Christians to be 'out there', living in God's world, joining in with all that God has planned.

In order to do this, God needs many different kinds of Christians, doing many different things. He needs men and women in the priesthood, in the episcopate, as doctors, as teachers, as carers, as mothers and fathers, as students, as politicians, as shop workers and as a whole host of other things. God cannot do what he needs to do without you. Your task is to find out what it is God is calling you to do and then to do it with all your heart, soul, mind and strength. As we have seen, it is likely to be a combination of vocations. You can't do everything. That much is clear. But you might be able to do more than you think, if the busyness doom-mongers are to be believed.

If you are busy and it's good, be busy. If not, make some radical choices about what you are meant to do – based on who you are. 'I have told you O man (and woman) what is good and what the Lord requires *of you*.' (Mic. 6.8). Don't allow yourself to be pushed into anyone's stereotypes. Be who God made you to be. It may be that you simply need the confidence to do *more* of the right things, in the strength of God. Once you have found what God is calling you to do, live it to the full.

Accept you can't do everything

The flip side of realizing we might be able to do more than we thought, is realizing also that we can't do everything and indeed that it would be wholly wrong to try. It is OK to want to do a lot of things and want to do them well, but it's not possible to do everything. It is not possible to have complete control of everything. That's God's job anyway.

There is a tendency for those of us who like to be busy to feel that the world would fall apart if we weren't. There is a strong urge in some of us (myself included) to have everything sorted, sewn up, done and dusted. As long as my house is orderly and my children neatly dressed with their teeth cleaned, as long as my shopping list is comprehensive and arranged in alphabetical order, as long as my sermons are wonderful and my prayer life immaculate and uplifting, as long as I carefully work out my calling and follow it nicely, then all will be well.

It may be that those of us who veer towards this way of thinking need to accept some mess in our lives sometimes, some unfinishedness, some incompleteness. David Runcorn writes: 'We must continually let go of our attempts to control and achieve our quest for wholeness for ourselves. Our story, with all its longings, will only be known as part of something much bigger and not yet revealed.'[4]

The South American archbishop and martyr Oscar Romero said this: 'We cannot do everything, and there is a sense of liberation in realizing that. This enables us to do something and do it well. It

4. Runcorn, 'Self-management', in *The Vicar's Guide*, p. 37.

may be incomplete, a step along the way, an opportunity for God's grace to enter and do the rest.'[5]

If we always have it all sewn up, under control and sorted, there would be no need for God. Those of us who like being busy are not very good at imperfection or weakness, but God encourages us to be weak in order that he might be strong. Even Paul, ever the successful busy-phile, speaks of how God has given him 'a thorn in his flesh' to stop him becoming conceited. We don't know exactly what this thorn was, but it leads the great Paul to recognize that God says to him:

'My grace is sufficient for you, for power is made perfect in weakness.' So I will boast all the more gladly about my weaknesses, so that power of Christ may dwell in me. Therefore, I am content with the weaknesses, insults, hardships, persecutions, and calamities for the sake of Christ; for whenever I am weak, then I am strong. (2 Cor. 12.9–10)

Typical of Paul to turn it all into strength and success anyway, but in the midst of the busyness, it is good to realise that we are not God – and we can't do it all.

One of the causes of busyness is the drive towards perfection, towards doing everything brilliantly. We have set the bar very high, but that is no surprise when we read Jesus's words that we should 'Be perfect, therefore, as your heavenly father is perfect' (Mt. 5.48). We misinterpret Jesus's words, however, if we take them to mean that we must continuously strive to be without fault. The original meaning of the world for 'perfect, *telios*, would have carried for its listeners, not the injunction to be flawless, but to be "finished, fulfilled, completed, accomplished, fully grown and mature" '.[6] 'Be fulfilled', we might better interpret it. We cannot *make* ourselves perfect, because only in Jesus are we *made* perfect: 'he has now reconciled in his fleshly body through death, so as to present you holy and blameless and irreproachable before him'

---

5. Quoted in Nick Cuthbert, *How to Survive and Thrive as a Church Leader* (Monarch Books, 2006), p. 113.
6. Evans, *Driven Beyond the Call of God*, p. 75.

(Col. 1.22). So our task is not to strive for perfection, but to be fulfilled and complete in the knowledge that in Christ we are made blameless, complete and whole before God.

Know you are loved

Remember that God loves you. Remember that God *likes* you. He's on your side. Your vocation comes out of what is best for you, as well as what God wants you to do in the world. Many people are so busy being God's servant that they forget to be his child.

In all our busyness it is essential that, whatever we do, we don't find our identity in *doing* but in *being* a child of God. As Mark Greene so clearly puts it:

> The Christian doesn't work to gain peace. On the contrary, we gain our peace from our relationship with God. Our *shalom*, our wholeness, is in Christ. It grows out of our relationship with him, from being in the vine, from the certainty of his love, on the basis of his promises to us. It is from the *shalom* we already have in Christ that we go out into the world. We don't run towards his rest, we run in his rest. We don't go to work to find our worth, we start work already in the knowledge of our worth in Christ. We don't go to work to gain status, we go to work with the status of the sons and daughters of the king of the universe.[7]

Have fun

Life is meant to be fun. In a busy life there should be plenty of opportunities to laugh at yourself and the world around you. I don't believe that we were put here on this planet to live our three

7. Greene, *Thank God it's Monday*, p. 143.

score years and ten in a cloud of misery and gloom. Yes, we are meant to think deeply and pray earnestly about busyness, about vocation, about relationships, about all of the things this book has been about. But we are also meant to be joyful. Not the false grin that we put on because we are tense but feel we ought to be happy, but the honest, real, deep joy of a heart that knows it is loved by God and is following God's ways – in the knowledge that 'the joy of the Lord is my strength' (Neh. 8:10).

So go on. . .